From time to time [illegible] only hearing about, but seeing and experiencing what's beyond this life. He has chosen Matthew and Nancy Botsford to be instruments to communicate to us the awful reality of hell and eternity without Christ. Through Matthew's being shot in the head and subsequent suffering, an urgent message of warning and hope has come to us. This testimony will change your life.

—Dan Slade, International Coordinator,
Partners in Harvest, Toronto, Canada

Matthew and Nancy Botsford have a first-hand testimony of what the future holds without God, and what it can become with Him! Their testimony offers real hope when it seems there is none to be found. You will be extremely blessed from hearing what God has done and what He will do for you!

— David White, Pastor of MorningStarFellowship
Church, Wilkesboro, North Carolina

In an instant life changed for Matt and Nancy Botsford. They were literally thrust into hell, both physically and spiritually. Yes, there is a hell— and yes there is redemption. This book is the story of their journey. Thank God, mercy triumphs over judgment!

— R. A. Beisner, author, pastor, and
retired NYS Supreme Court Justice

A DAY IN HELL
The sky is the limit
no more limits on you
& family

God is breaking
forth $, prosperity
time to do His Works
in His might
- It is all going to
be EASY simply
w/ one or two bumps
in your journey
OH BUT GOD is
OH BUT GOD gets
the GLORY Well HONOR

A Day in Hell

Death to Life to Hope

Nancy Botsford

Tate Publishing & *Enterprises*

A Day In Hell

Published by Tate Publishing & Enterprises, LLC
127 E. Trade Center Terrace | Mustang, Oklahoma 73064 USA
1.888.361.9473 | www.tatepublishing.com

Tate Publishing is committed to excellence in the publishing industry. The company reflects the philosophy established by the founders, based on Psalm 68:11,
"The Lord gave the word and great was the company of those who published it."

Cover design by Chris Webb
Interior design by Kristen Verser

Published in the United States of America

ISBN: 978-1-61663-251-9
1. Religion, Christian Life, Spiritual Growth
2. Religion, Christian Life, Inspirational
10.05.03

DEDICATION

TO MY INCREDIBLE HUSBAND WHO BESTOWS CONFIDENCE, WISDOM, AND VALIANT HONOR...I LOVE YOU.

ACKNOWLEDGMENTS

We want to thank all the family and friends who stuck close in the hardest, darkest of times, lending love and support in the most critical moments, whether they knew it or not; for praying when things were bleak; for crying when things went wrong; for hugging and laughing as slivers of light were seen. We want to thank all the professional and medical people who tirelessly devoted themselves to enhancing our welfare and Matthew's extensive physical and cognitive rehabilitation efforts over the years. Most assuredly, thanks to our heavenly Father, God, and His Son, Jesus Christ, who lovingly kept us close to Their hearts and hands, even when we didn't know it or acknowledge Them. We love You, Daddy, our heavenly Father.

In order for the full power of this testimonial story to be felt, for all the dynamics to be expressed, you the reader will find two points of view: one of the injured, Matthew, noted as *[Matthew's dialogue]*; and one of the spouse, Nancy, noted as *[Nancy's dialogue]*. You will also see headings and chapters noting *As recounted by Matthew* and *As recounted by Nancy*. We have made great efforts to distinguish for you the reader whose point of view you are reading at all times so that you can see how the saving grace of our dear Lord can and will empower you in and through all of your life's trials and tribulations; whether inflicted by others or even self-inflicted. Jesus is the way, the truth, and the life (John 14:6, NKJV). Names other than Matthew and Nancy have been changed to protect personal identities.

PREFACE

A Day in Hell is the riveting, true-life account of one man's descent to the bowels of hell after dying from a gunshot wound to the head in March of 1992 while on a business trip to Atlanta, Georgia and the true, wholehearted prayer of love by his newly wedded wife, calling out, "Lord, bring back my husband in whatever condition he may be. Just bring him back, and I promise to stay with him for the rest of my life." The damaging effects of the 9 mm bullet tearing into the brain were severe, resulting in paralysis and extensive cognitive damage. The organ harvesters were lining up for his eventual death while he lay comatose. But Matthew survived, waking up twenty-seven days later, unbeknown to all those surrounding him of how the actual hand of God came and pulled him from his cell in hell and God told him, "It's not your time." *A Day in Hell* is a story flooded with hope and inspiration as this young couple figures out how to plot their new life with such tragic memories and the never-ending challenges that the cognitive and physical paralysis from the brain injury brought on in a world designed for the non-disabled. Feel the faith, hope, and love as you read of their incredible, turn-around journey to life and Jesus. Walk with them on the golden path that it is built upon the ever generous love of the Father. The love of our heavenly Daddy exudes from the story lines. You'll agree after reading this that our God is definitely a good God, regardless of present circumstances, and He always has a plan for you—tragedy to triumph for a world that is seeking something real and lasting, seeking even to find out who they are; even seeking what their purpose is in life, often wondering what's beyond this life. Let this story outline a parallel that one can be encouraged by to know that there is more than just surviving. You can thrive when fueled by His love from on high.

FIRE ONE

"Fire one, baby! Fire one, baby!"

Screams came from everywhere. Nine millimeter shots rang from every direction. World War Three started on the streets of Atlanta, Georgia. People ran, scattering in every direction, filling the streets and the restaurant with panic and fear. Utter chaos ensued. The shooter stood on the corner of the cracked concrete sidewalk with a cool chill in the air. He squeezed the trigger of an Uzi machine gun, anger pumping through his veins, spraying bullets into the crowd outside of the building.

Matthew was hit from behind, the 9 mm bullet piercing the back right side of his head, instantly knocking him to the ground, blood pouring from his head as Matthew gasped. His brother bent down to hear Matthew's last breaths.

Joe began yelling, "Help! Someone! My brother has been shot! Help! He is dying! Help!"

An employee from inside the restaurant watching the outside surveillance camera ran outside to Matthew and began CPR until the ambulance arrived. As this was happening, shots rang out again. This time, the shooters were in an SUV and driving past the front of the building, shooting everywhere. People ran for cover, dodging behind parked cars. Others ran to the side entrance, hoping to find safety. Alas, the heavy, steel, roll-down door was shut and locked to protect inside guests.

Steve, the other business associate who was with Matthew and his brother, pounded on the door, shouting, “Let us in! Let us in! There are people out here!”

They ran for cover, crouching down low between the closest cars as 9 mm bullets were singing over their heads, ricocheting off of the metallic bodies.

One bystander turned to Steve on the ground and said, “We made it, dude.”

Steve didn’t respond, so he rolled Steve over; half of his face was blown off from the lone bullet that hit him from behind as they ran. That chilling night, the twenty-first of March, 1992, with dozens of people outside the restaurant, two got hit, and two died.

[Nancy's dialogue]

Matthew, Joe, and Steve were expecting this outdoor product convention to kick-start the spring sales for the entire year. New outdoor power equipment and sales incentives always showed for a profitable year for them and the business. As usual, they would leave the day before for travel and to check into a hotel. Matthew always got excited before any conference. He was packing the night before, Friday. I was anxious and already missed him. In the back of my mind, I felt uneasy and did not want him to go. I said nothing. That night was a date. We ate steak, baked potatoes, and salad and had a glass of wine and bubble bath. It was great. The morning of Matthew's departure, Matthew was ready to go, and I was still feeling that something was wrong. *It must be my nerves,* I thought. Or was it?

That night, usually, I would get a phone call from Matthew that he was checked into the hotel and given a number to reach him and told that he loves me and that he misses me too. It was 9:30 p.m. and no call. *Oh, his plane got delayed,* I told myself. It was 10:00 p.m. Still no call, and that wrong feeling was beginning to heighten. Eleven p.m. I was getting scared. I fell asleep. I woke up at 2:00 a.m. with a scared, sick feeling. Then the phone rang. It was Matthew's dad. His voice was shaky.

I asked, "Is he alive?"

Dad's voice cracked and he said, "Yes, but Matthew has been shot. Mom and I are flying to Atlanta."

I said, "I am going too."

I remember hanging up the phone, breathing very heavily, and being totally paralyzed with fear—not even aware of my own breathing.

I somehow got to the office down the hall and saw the stacked bills paid and sealed with address labels on them. Early that day, I wrote and paid all the bills. This was not normal. Usually, I would pay late or on the fly. For some reason, I paid them all; and if I had had stamps, they would have been on them too. I always knew things (word of knowledge) but I never understood the gift inside of me. I called my parents, who were on their vacation, and my brother, who lived in a nearby town, and I remember calling my sister and brother-in-law in Florida with the news and explaining what I knew. Then, behind me, Matthew's sister arrived at my home.

She stood in the office doorway with tears in her eyes, shaking her head, saying, "No. It does not look good."

And she was there for me. I thought to myself, *What is happening?* I hung up the phone and said, "I must pack for the trip." I stood in front of my closet, blank with what to pack, pulling things that I thought I needed. *A suit jacket? Why?* I pondered. I heard a car pull into the driveway. As I stepped out, I realized that it was snowing, blowing, and drifting. *What else?* I thought.

As we were driving the forty-five-minute trip to the airport, I found out that Steve had been shot too and that he was in surgery; but I heard nothing about Matthew. Calls would come in, but not about Matthew. I sat quietly, wondering if we could go any faster as we crawled through the snow drifts due to a Michigan blizzard and treacherous road conditions. Two hours later, we finally got to the airport. We went to get our tickets, and I noticed that Matthew's parents did not have any bags. It did not occur to me why until later on. At this time, it was five o'clock in the morning. We still had an hour to board the plane.

I thought, *Why don't we hire a private jet? This is an emergency. My husband has been shot. Help, someone,* I scream in my mind. On the red-eye flight, what was only a two-hour trip took forever. Time seemed to stand still. Matthew's parents and I sat in our assigned seats, saying nothing to each other. Yet each one of us was wondering, *What, where, when, how, and why?*

The taxi ride from the airport to the hospital was grueling—forty-five minutes in silence, my heart beating faster with every mile closer to the hospital. We finally arrived at the emergency exit. I quickly got out of the taxi, and I saw Matthew's brother, Joe, walking outside to greet us. The look on our faces must have been terrible. Because of the look on Joe's face, I yelled out, fearing what the answer would be.

"Is he alive, and where is he?"

We all were quickly ushered inside, walking through corridors and around corners. We stopped at a small room with a few chairs and a table with a lamp. We were directed to put our few belongings there as we were ushered down other corridors and hallways until we entered the intensive care unit (ICU). There, an attendant for the ICU area wanted to prepare us for Matthew's condition. All I kept saying was, "Where is he? I want to see my husband." As the attendant spoke, that sick, terrifying, fearful, paralyzing feeling was overwhelming me. "His head is all wrapped up with gauze and swollen. He is in a coma, so he is totally paralyzed and on a respirator, and he is critical." None of this prepared us for what we would see. As we walked into the ICU station, I heard beeps from monitors and breathing respirators from every room. The main area was a circular desk that nurses and doctors entered in and out of with the eight glass patient rooms all around. As we all walked toward his room, in my peripheral vision, I saw others all on respirators, hooked up to beeping monitors. Then the nurse gestured at the number 3. I saw Matthew's name, and my heart was pounding with every step, not believing that this was happening, that this was actually real. Then I saw him all bandaged up, hooked up to wires and lines and a respirator that breathed for him. His head was three times the normal size, with his right side swollen even more. His right eye was protruding from under the gauze wrap. It was horrifying. His face was totally disfigured. The only way that I knew it was Matthew for certain was by his wedding ring. My knees got weak, and my mouth went dry. I stood in shock, trying to believe what I was seeing, trying to breathe. Matthew's parents left quickly from the shock of seeing their son. This was devastating for everyone.

I stood by Matthew's side. Time stood still as I looked at every wire and line and even some monitor bolted in the top of his head. Then a nurse came in to explain all the gadgets hooked up to my husband. The respiratory nurse came in quickly, removing lines; and she started to suction out Matthew's lungs. It was such a horrifying noise, and my husband was gasping. My knees buckled under me, and I grabbed the side of the hospital bed to catch my fall.

The nurse said, "Oh, you never saw this? Well, we do this quite often, and you will get used to it."

It seemed like hours went by before I saw anyone but nurses come and go in and out of the eight rooms. Once in awhile, I would see my father-in-law looking though the glass window; then I saw Steve's parents rush in to the main area, hugging and crying. I looked at the nurse, and she just looked sad and shook her head, which told me that Steve did not make it. Again, my mind began spinning, not believing or able to comprehend the reality of murder and my husband lying in a coma, fighting for every breath. Steve was at another hospital close by. He was on the respirator, hooked up to life support, needing his wife to arrive from out of state. As additional information came though, Steve's wife was snowed in up north in Michigan. Steve's parents had to authorize the pulling of the plug, devastated as hour by hour passed. They were so brave.

As I began to understand what monitors did what and what all the wires and lines were for, I was informed of the doctor overseeing the case and that he was the neurosurgeon who worked on Matthew many hours before and that he would speak to us with an update soon. In the meantime, there were three fugitives out there somewhere in Atlanta, so the hospital was in an automatic shutdown, where everyone was questioned and police and news broadcasters were all over, hanging out in the lobbies and in the sitting areas; we were told to stay in the ICU area. Also, with the fugitives not caught yet, Joe was in danger. He saw what the shooter on foot looked like. My parents arrived sometime around noon. Everyone was trying to understand the facts as they would trickle in. I remember that reporters were pretending to be family members to try to get into the ICU area to get any information of the victims, anything at all. It was crazy, and then it was time to meet and get an update about Matthew, finally. One of the nurses took me to a small room, and inside was my brother-in-law and the doctor, a handsome man in his early forties, of Indian descent.

I asked, "Where are Matthew's parents?"

Joe said, "Sit down and hear what the doctor has to tell you."

That sick feeling came again, and my heart dropped into my stomach. I was scared, really, really scared.

"Hello, Mrs. Botsford."

I choked out, "Nancy. Please call me Nancy."

Joe reached across the table and grabbed my hand. The doctor explained how Matthew came in at around midnight to the emergency room for surgery and how the doctor took out the damaged brain and skin, nerves the size of a grapefruit; and, of all things, he even said that Matthew flat-lined three times.

I thought, *Died?* Again my head was spinning, trying to gather thoughts, trying to breathe, looking at Matthew's brother. He was crushed.

Then the doctor took a deep breath and said, "If your husband makes it through the night, it is a thirty percent chance. If he makes it though the night with the severe brain injury, he might be paralyzed and be in a wheelchair and, not sure of the extent of the brain injury, he might even be put into an institution."

My mind was screaming, *What? What is happening? I need Matthew, my best friend.* I was so alone.

The doctor suggested that Matthew might not live, so a team of organ donors were just in the other room, waiting to harvest his organs for other recipients to have a chance for life. All over the world, people were on standby. At that moment, I remembered seeing out of my peripheral vision a room to the right of the ICU area with five people all holding red and white coolers, anxiously looking at us as we entered the ICU. I looked at Joe and then looked at the doctor for hope. I saw none.

I walked out of the meeting with the doctor, shocked. Every emotion was numb. I was screaming inside, needing my husband, my best friend; but I could not talk to him or even feel our connection—blankness, nothing.

I looked and saw my dad in the main lobby talking to a woman. She had a recorder shoved in his face.

I stormed over to her and, with my emotions going wild, said in a firm, raised voice, "Leave my father alone. You do not belong here."

She persisted.

I, in a louder voice, said, "Get out of here!"

This got the attention of the nearby police officer, and she was escorted out before I would go off full force. This put me over to the edge. I began to lose my sense of reality; so, to not attract more reporters, I retreated to the ICU area, and an organ donor harvester shoved a legal document in my face to sign for them to harvest my husband's organs before he was declared dead. I believe I yelled "no."

Nancy's Encounter with Jesus

[Nancy's dialogue]

I remember going down an empty corridor. I was shaking, trembling. I stopped to catch my breath, and I saw blackness in front of me, down at my feet. It was getting larger all around. I felt like I was losing all sense of reality, losing control of my mind and my senses. I was numb and fearful. I was losing it. I remember that I started to fall forward into the blackness of oblivion. I had no control over anything. Nothing, and then I felt a hand firmly grab my right shoulder and pull me back from the blackness. I turned around to see who it was, if it was a family member or, worse, a reporter. No one was there — nothing. But then, instantly, I knew that it was Jesus who grabbed me. I knew it. Every cell in my body instantly knew Him, and I just could not see Him.

I ran back to Matthew's room. He was all bandaged up, in a coma, on a respirator that was breathing for him. I was standing on the front right side of the bed.

I looked up and said, "Lord." I am not saved at this point. "Lord, bring back my husband. Bring back who he is, his heart, his personality. Even if he is in a wheelchair, I promise to stay with him forever."

Due to my cry from deep within my heart, a shift in the spiritual realm began; the heavenly courts were opened for adjudication.

[Matthew's dialogue]

The Lord always says to me during or after I, Matthew testify of my experience, getting shot dying and going to hell.

He says, "There is so much more to know regarding what I (God) had to go through to pull you out of hell." He went on to reveal to me that there were legal issues at hand, for without a legality of things, righteousness and justice would never be able to reign on Earth. Remember, "His will be done on earth as it is in heaven" (Matthew 6:10, NKJV).

As Nancy finished the plea, "I promise to stay with him forever," those words were formed into a formal petition that was handed into Jesus's right hand, tears still dripping from it.

As Jesus approached the heavenly courts, two massive, gold-hinged, antiquated wood doors before Him parted. There were no handles or door knob present, only a large keyhole in the rightmost door. In strode Jesus, adorned in a full-length, golden white, luminescent garb. A wide, shimmering, gold chord belt about His waist cinched firm to gather the flowing luminous white material into proper form. A deep, wide hood came to rest gently upon His broad back after being removed prior to crossing the threshold of the court room, revealing His dark, golden brown hair, reminiscent of a lion's mane. In His right hand, He clutched the scroll rolled tightly. "Father," Jesus announced.

All eyes in the heavenly court were riveted upon Jesus. The evil ones in the courts became instantly enraged and agitated, snarling at the interruption of the Lamb, throwing insults and accusations at Him like daggers and spears.

"What's He doing here?" one called out.

A second echoed his dagger with an unintelligible insult of his own while the good ones in the courts expressed their mercy just through the respect afforded in their countenance toward Jesus as He entered and began His deliberate approach toward the Judge's high throne, upon which God was seated, cherubim and seraphim on each side.

Jesus continued, clutching the scroll in His right hand. "Father, we have new evidence that has just come into my hands that bears Your immediate attention."

"Yes." God breathed His answer in such a way that His single voice filled the chambers. "Show Me, My Son." (God already knew what His Son was holding, for He is the Alpha and Omega, the First and the Last, Omniscient Being, meaning all-knowing, and Omnipotent One, meaning all-powerful.) "For You know that according to the law, Matthew must go to hell, even though I do not like to have to do it." Father God continued speaking. "It is the law and the grace that We have established from the foundations of the world when all was but chaos." God zeroed in on His Son. "He did not know You, the slain Lamb, My only Son, upon his death."

"Yes, Father. I know," Jesus responded remorsefully. Jesus handed my wife's petition for my life to His dad.

God reached out to retrieve the rolled scroll without moving. God unrolled the scroll, noticing every detail of it. It was still moist with my wife's tears. After a moment's pause, God proudly announces, "Well now, this does shed light on Our decision, doesn't it?"

The evil ones rose in the chambers in agony and angst, their pain plainly evidenced in their contorted faces and disambiguated forms.

God continued. "Now I can legally penetrate satan's realm and retrieve Matthew from his dire confines in hell."

The good ones shouted, "Hallelujah! Hallelujah! Hallelujah! Worthy is the Lamb! Worthy is the Lamb!" Beautiful light emanates from their voices, filling the court room with a symphony of sound and light.

Yet on the other side of the court, great discord ensued, trying to mount on the evil ones' part; but for only a brief moment, for God is not mocked. It is His courtroom and His throne room. One look from the throne, one shifting of the Father's attention toward the perpetrators of the disorderly conduct, and reverential fear was brought back to the court room with a whoosh of sound.

[Matthew's dialogue cont'd] After my wife got touched on her right shoulder by Jesus, she was then empowered by the Son to plead aloud with her whole heart, "Lord, please bring back my husband like he always was. Just keep Matthew, wheelchair or not, but bring back who he was." I emphasize "whole heart," for to be heard in the heavenly courts, one must not be *fragmented in heart.* Jesus, our adjudicator, heard that desperate plea from her whole heart and was implored to go before His Daddy, God the Father, and ask for me on behalf of my wife's plea, for she had the legal right to plea for my life in the heavenly courts due to our marriage covenant. Our marriage covenant is, in fact, a biblical covenant or seal that creates the basis for the legal argument. Then and only then was God able to act out of His divine mercy and side up with my wife and pluck me from the dark confines of hell.

I believe that we are both examples of what's been termed prevenient grace. God enabled her, through the touch of His Son, Jesus; and God enabled me through His touch upon my heart in hell to only desire to seek Them (Father, Son, and Holy Spirit) all the days of our lives. In John 6:44 (NKJV), Jesus says, "No one can come to me, unless the Father who sent me draws him; and I will raise him up at the last day." In my own words, God calls first.

They (Father, Son, and Spirit) knew what our decisions would be once we were of the right mind to make a decision. That's not to say that They protected us in some mysterious way from still having the ability to choose that which would lead us away from Them, but the divine team did know we would choose Them over the things of this present and passing away world (1 John 2:17, NKJV).

A DAY IN HELL
AS RECOUNTED BY MATTHEW

[Matthew's dialogue]

I felt a hot, needle-like pierce, excruciatingly painful, for a brief instant at the top of my head; and then utter darkness enveloped me as if thick, black ink had been poured over my eyes—so black, so thick that it encompassed my very being, having a palpable nature to it. Reaching out only proved to me that I was actually contained in some sort of cell; reaching to my left and my right, up and down proved the black endlessness of my confines. No walls, floor, or ceiling could I discover; yet confined I was. The total eclipse of all light was just one extent of my misery. Evil was present on all sides. It was an ever-present form of evil, bringing me to the realization that no good was to be found here.

Cold permeated to the very morrow of my bones—an icy, water-type cold, in that it surrounded all of me, inside and out. It was in my lungs and stomach and head. I felt as if I had surely swallowed the icy cold waters beneath the polar ice cap. A liquid cold that fully encapsulated and fully surrounded me. Next came the realization that this thing was eternal in nature. Time was of no consequence here, confined in this evil cell of darkness. A cell in hell—yes, a cell in hell was where I was being kept. And I was naked—not in the sense of "Oh my, am I embarrassed." No. I mean stripped of all worldly things, stripped of everything personal and dear to me—no coverings of any sort, just stark naked. Naked can be defined as having no protecting or concealing cover, and that befits my experience very well. I was totally unprotected and unconcealed against the evil elements in hell and in full view of the terrifying demonic elements themselves. I could feel the actual pressure of evil pressing against my body. All my senses flooded with fear, hopelessness, and dread. All I knew was bad. All I knew was evil. All I knew was dread and doom. All that I knew was these experiences. No life did I feel. My heart did not beat circulating lifeblood through my body. There were no thoughts of anything else. Totally encompassing fear, terror, and dread filled my very being. Actually, there were no thoughts at all. I had no thoughts of anything but hopelessness and dread, doom and gloom. No good thoughts of my beloved wife. No thoughts of my past. No thoughts for my future because that would have given rise to the possibility for hope to bloom. Actually, there was no breathing either. Though I was fully present in bodily form, I did not breathe—no inhalation or exhalation. There was no air present. There were no smells, either good or bad, just stagnant nonexistence. It was a state of eternal nonexistence except for the fear and dread and hopelessness that gripped and squashed my heart. I refer these things to my heart, for that is where these things were experienced. In my heart, these things were experienced. Deadly silence filled the air—not just silence, but the nonexistence of all sounds. The environment was stagnant. Then, from high above, in the topmost right-hand corner of my sight, a protuberance began to appear, as if you were to slowly push your finger into a thick, heavy, black garbage bag. A massive index finger appeared. It burst through. It was a man's index finger, evidenced by the masculine fingerprint and crevices I could see. This finger was massive in my sight. Slowly and very methodically, I watched it descend toward me with the entirety of the hand coming into full view once it seemingly breached that upper and outer pitch black barrier. It was a right hand. I gazed upon the palm and the underside of the slightly inward-curved thumb and fingers as they approached me. Oddly enough, from my position below, I also could see the back of this hand, including the throbbing veins that ran along the topmost of the hand toward the fingers. The veins seemed to be carrying life itself in them, lifeblood. Short, blackish hairs curled about themselves while some stood on end, straight, about the breadth of the hand. I saw the lined knuckle joints with small tendons stretching atop just like yours and mine. Yet this hand was so massive, so strong in appearance, so full of life. The palm, the underside that approached me, appeared cracked and creviced from what looked like the affects of great age and great works, antiquated yet simultaneously gentle and supple. Following behind and from without, brilliant white light shone. The brilliance and purity of the light seemed warlike in its overtaking of the blackness. Finely engrained, glistening, silvery-white feathers entered from the same entry point of the index finger and swirled about my confines in cyclonic fashion. For the first time, sound was to be heard. I heard an ethereal sound as the glistening feathers filled the cell, surrounding my entirety—a symphony of sound and praise, strings mostly. The hand descended to me with the light shining about it, emanating from it; and the feathers simultaneously swirled about following with its descent. This hand gently wrapped itself around my whole body, my back and waist lying somewhere in the palm area of the hand. I began an ascent as soon as I was grasped by this hand. It felt like an elevator ride in that it was straight up, no deviations to the left or the right, just straight up and quick, right through the music that was permeating the cell; then I heard a commanding voice that came from everywhere all at once. I even heard it inside of me. It sounded like a thunderous clap of lightening, a great wind and white water rapids all rolled together, saying, "It's not your time!" In an instant, all the fear was gone. All the blackness lifted. Cold vanished. Evil disappeared. This voice seemed to be beyond the three-dimensional realm we live in. It was as though it came from outside of time and not only spoke to me but spoke to the very existence of what enveloped me. It was obvious that my confines and all of its hellish characteristics were subservient to this voice by their prompt exit. No attempts were made to wage a battle or complaint. I knew at this point that everything was going to be okay. That's all I knew, that everything was going to be okay.

I have been asked, "How or why would this happen to you?" My answer: "I did not have Jesus as my Savior when, upon dying from the gunshot wound to my head, I went straight to hell."

Others have asked, "So, what was this hand, and where did the hand lift you to?"

The answer to the first question is, "The hand of God," and the answer to the second part is, "My Spirit was lifted out of hell so that my physical body could be revived, for without Spirit, we are mere dead flesh. There is nothing I can do to separate me from the Love of my Father, God." Even in the times of my stupidity of disobedience and sin, my Father will never separate His Love from me, (Hebrews 13:5, Deuteronomy 31:6, NKJV). After hearing His voice, I knew that I was going to be okay. I didn't know what that meant, but all was okay. I think, looking back now, that my Spirit man knew what had happened, that the very hand of God had rescued me from the eternal pit of hell, and that everything was good now. My Spirit man could now rejoice in Him, the Father of all creation. What had to follow was the fleshly man, the soul part of me sometime in the future.

[Nancy's dialogue]

What happened in the worldly courts nine months later was quite different. Every day of the court proceedings, we would see the men who shot Matthew and murdered Steve in an elevator that would transport Matthew, me, and a guard to the court room. Because Matthew was in the wheelchair, that was the only way up. Go figure. God had a plan. I recall the elevator having a nasty stench to it, like all the lies, deceit, and murder had permeated the very walls; and we had to ride up in it every day. We would see the men with anger and hatred in their eyes; but by the end of the murder trial ten days later, they had shame and could not even look up at us as we all waited for that old elevator to carry us up to the court room for the final decision. First, the inmates would travel up that ancient elevator; and then we would enter into that same elevator that just had the inmates. Sometimes there would be a delay because the inmates would fight one another. I am sure they were fighting about the details to reveal of what truly happened in the day surrounding the shooting on March 21, 1992. That frightful day changed the lives of so many. The negative effects continue to ripple outward in some to this very day; people we know personally and even people we do not know. It is endless on the lives that were affected by this horrifying turn of events. The far reaching psychological and physical effects of such a tragic event are staggering; consuming some with rage, revenge, and un-forgiveness. Yet if a person looks close enough with a pure heart they will see the hand of God fast at work. I remember that all the guards would be happy to see us because we had hope—a smile when everyone else was upset, angry, and indifferent. Also inside the court room, I remember that the grandfather of one of the shooters would open the heavy oak wood door to the court room for Matthew and me to enter every day. He had such a sad and remorseful look on his face that told the whole story. But Matthew and I had total, 100 percent forgiveness from day one that now I know flowed out of us and affected everyone even the shooters.

The shooting occurred on March 21, 1992; the murder trial was not until November, nine months later. Matthew was still in the wheelchair, and he could stand for a moment or two. The trial was held in the Atlanta, Georgia, downtown court building. I remember riding in an unmarked police car through downtown Atlanta; and upon arriving at the court building, sheriffs would line the street with semi-automatic rifles, ready for warfare. It was like a scene in a scary movie, and we were the main characters. Every day, the prosecuting attorneys, our lawyers, witnesses, and us would all meet to discuss what would happen for that court session. Each day would bring us closer to the final decision. I remember that after about eight days, it started to look like a mistrial would happen and we all would have to do the entire court testifying and work all over again. It was a very intense day and night.

Finally, the judge stepped up through all the confusion; she took control over the preceding, and one man who turned state's evidence was freed and the other two inmates, after ten days, were sentenced to life (which is a minimum of twenty-five years).

The worldly courts here on this earth were set up by man with the hope of Godly principles; but the heavenly courts have only the one judge, and the outcome is quite different than here on earth.

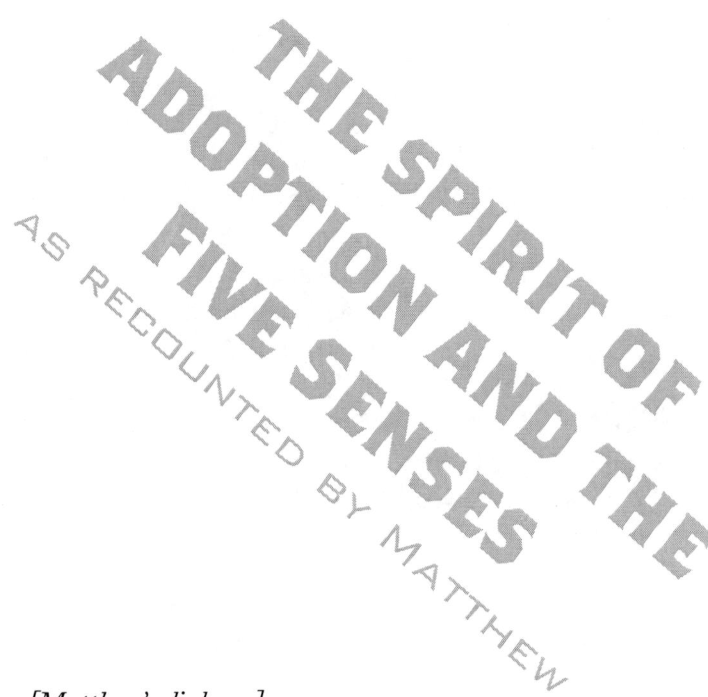

[Matthew's dialogue]

I heard, I saw, I smelled, I felt, and I tasted the wrath and evil of hell; I heard, I saw, I smelled, I felt and I tasted the goodness and love of God. Psalm 34:8 (NKJV) says, "Oh, taste, and see, that the Lord is good." These direct dichotomies of the kingdom of Satan and the kingdom of God are what led me to Him through His Spirit of adoption. I left my orphanhood behind after this experience, choosing the better, to be called a child of God. Romans 8:15 (NKJV) speaks of "receiving the Spirit of adoption by whom we cry out, Abba Father." *How* do we receive this spirit of adoption? You receive it just like I did, by saying yes to Jesus, thereby embracing His Father's love. My experience in being adopted by the Father is one of a quest, whereas the Father views it as a finished work the moment we come to Him; so this is not to say we should neglect our priceless salvation. No. Certainly not. In fact, we should earnestly press on with authentic, genuine fervor and our whole heart continuously. I like Apostle Paul's remarks. "Brethren, I do not count myself to have apprehended; but one thing I do, forgetting those things which are behind and reaching forward to those things which are ahead, I press toward the goal for the prize of the upward call of God in Christ Jesus" (Philippians 3:13–14, NKJV). *Where* do we receive the spirit of adoption? I believe it is something that must be received into our hearts; for if it lies only in our minds, we truly will never become the sons and daughters of God that He intends us to become. It is the experiential that moves things from our minds into our hearts. So *how* does a person receive the *experiential* of God without taking a bullet to the head, so to speak? It's probably exactly that which must be, a proverbial bullet to the head. When does the Word of God become alive to us? The Holy Spirit will quicken the Word of God in our spirits if we have the Holy Spirit abiding in us. We must not make the mistake thinking that the Holy Spirit has somehow departed from us (Acts 1:4–5, Acts 2:4, NKJV). Verse 8 in Acts, chapter one says, "You shall receive power when the Holy Spirit has come upon you; and you shall be witnesses to Me in Jerusalem, and in all of Judea and Samaria, and to the end of the Earth."

We need the Holy Spirit to, in fact, fulfill any of the instructions from the Lord Himself. Jesus says in John 14:16 (NKJV) that "I, Jesus, will pray the Father and He will give you another Helper, that He may abide with you forever …" That sounds to me like Holy Spirit is here right now and forever more until the end of the age. In fact, it is He, the Holy Spirit, who will guide you into all truth; for He will not speak on His own authority, but whatever He hears (hears from whom? Hears from the Father Himself) He will speak, and He will tell you things to come. Jesus goes on to say that Holy Spirit will take of what is His (all things that the Father has are mine) and give it to us (John 16:13–15, NKJV). This all means that it is the Holy Spirit who will give us/declare to us what God has given to His Son, Jesus. I think that's pretty awesome that we, in fact, are given all things that the Father has. I remember before my injury and before I knew Jesus that the Bible seemed to be just a bunch of words and mumbo jumbo. It didn't make any sense to me, and I felt nothing when I did look in it. On the contrary, when I pick up the Bible today or even think about a scripture or even the principle of a scripture, my heart jumps with the anticipation of what Daddy (I refer to God the Father as my Daddy to indicate the intimacy in which He and I share. I view myself as but a small child looking to Him, my Daddy for everything I need, my daily bread so to speak. [Matthew 18:3, NKJV]). This experience with God leads me to trust Him in everything. If the Father could come into the very depths of hell for my rescue, surely He can take care of me in any circumstance that this life throws at me. Likewise, it is for you, the reader. Our Father in heaven is more than able to take care of you, regardless of your present circumstances. Even when all looks black and bleak and hopeless, with no end in sight, Father can and will do for you all you have need of because our Father is a good Daddy and He knows what we have need of before we even ask (Matthew 6:8 NKJV). He knows the beginning from the end and will intervene in the right time and in the right way (Isaiah 46:10, NKJV). Trust Him, for He is trustworthy. Believe in Him, for He is believable. Have faith because He is faithful. "But, without faith it is impossible to please Him, for he who comes to God must believe that He is, and that He is a rewarder of those that diligently seek Him" (Hebrews 11:6, NKJV). It's not even a matter of having faith in Him. "What?" you say. Yes. As I said, it's not really a matter of having faith *in* God; it's a matter of having the faith *of* God. Faith *in* God can be merely knowledge. Faith *of* God has to be a heart thing. This is way beyond just having faith in God in our heads. When it's in our hearts, our actions in daily life will be controlled by the faith of God. A person's heart reveals the person. I say faith *of* God, for faith came from God in the first place, like Sarah judging God faithful on His promise for a son (Hebrews 11:11b, NKJV). "How do I trust a God that seems so far away at times?" you might ask.

"He is not a faraway God," I answer. "He is as close, if not closer than, the nose on your face." I don't like that analogy, but I think you get the point. Just to reiterate more eloquently, Jesus lives inside those (John 17:21b, NKJV) who have accepted Him as Savior, and He is seated at the right hand of God, making intercession for us night and day (Romans 8:34, Colossians 3:1, Hebrews 7:25, NKJV). That makes me feel pretty good, knowing that the Son of God is sitting in heaven, interceding for His saints here on earth. All the kingdoms of this world will perish, but His will last forever. Seek His face today. If you seek Him, He will make sure you find Him (1 Chronicles 28:9, The Message). The trials and challenges of life will only serve to make your heart more in tune with the Father, provided that we do not harden ours toward His. I have plenty of reasons to harden my heart toward our God but have come to realize that there was (is) a special impartation, a special transmission from God for these situations—for you might be needing His grace, a special impartation to believe Him for your healing, for your marriage, for your family, for your finances. If you trust Him and do not doubt but do all you can do to further your relationship with Jesus, His Father, and the Holy Spirit, you will find that once the trial is over, or even during it, you would have had it no other way. My trust in our Daddy and His Son, Jesus, was first set up in my cell in hell. Yours will be set as you pursue Him too. Just do not harden your hearts like in the days of Moses regarding most of the Israelites.

Seek Him like a child meaning come to Him with no pretenses of who you think He is except for a wonderful, loving Daddy who happened to also create the entire world, universe, and whole human race. Now that's a big Daddy. I think you will agree. Once you find the simplicity in that He is pure love and all He does out of love, the deep will be yours to explore with Him. Let's journey into His depths.

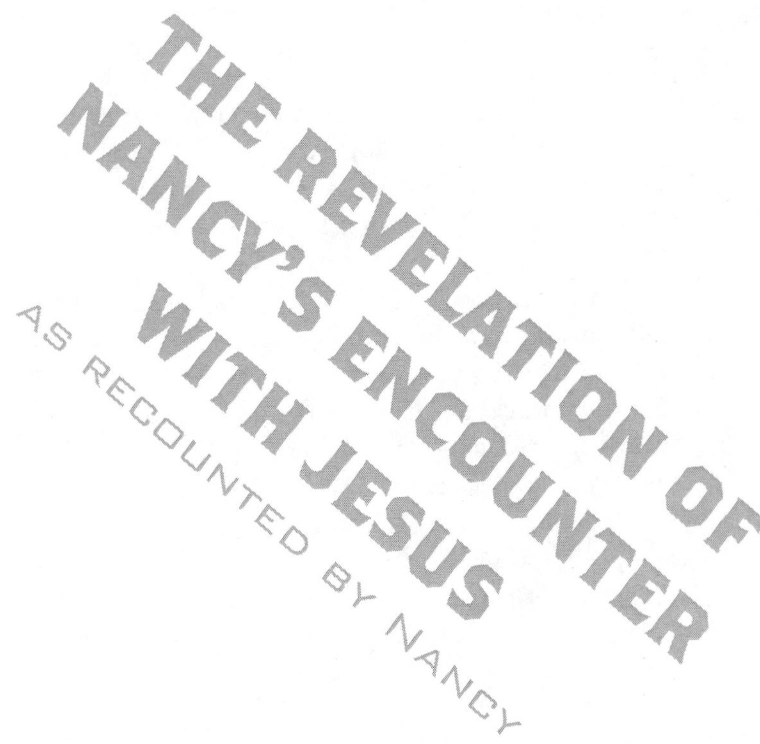

[Nancy's dialogue]

The right hand of Jesus that saved me from utter darkness was firm but gentle, strong but soft. As I turned around, it was as if a suitor asked me to dance for the rest of my life. I remember that as a little girl, I always loved to twirl around and around. Today, I love to dance for the Lord every time I have a chance—during worship; in the kitchen, cooking. Just imagine dancing with Jesus every moment of every day. Here is a wrench in theology, that one touch from Jesus began my salvation and gave me the ultra authority to petition for my husband's life and Jesus took that petition to the heavenly courts, where God was and is seated, and my petition from Jesus's hand changed the course of the judgment.

Amazing. In an earlier chapter, the entire vision Matthew had will enlighten you. After I said, "Lord," at the touch from Jesus, a reverence of the Lord and surrender was instantaneous. After I petitioned for Matthew's life, I was feeling overwhelmed, so I went to a small hall restroom. I knelt down into a crouched position, fearfully shaking and crying; then I felt warmth that covered me like a blanket. I felt the warmth all through my body, in every cell. The fear left, and a comfort beyond words flooded me. I stopped crying. I felt peace in a way that I never ever felt before. I felt calm, encouraged, peaceful, strong, rested. From that moment on, I was able to make many critical life decisions. I was at peace. At that moment, I still did not have the full realization of my encounter with Jesus Christ yet.

ADOPTION

AS RECOUNTED BY NANCY

[Nancy's dialogue]

March 21, 1992 was our day of adoption for me and Matthew. On this day, our names were written in the Book of Life. Forever, from this day forward, we were children of God, a daughter and a son of God with full access to all the privileges of the royal kingdom of the Almighty God, ruler, creator of all things, the Alpha and Omega. He is Jehovah (1 Kings 18:24, NKJV). Also, in Exodus 6:3 (NKJV), God Almighty is El-Shaddai and Yahweh—the redemptive and many, many more names of God. The privileges include royal robe, signet ring, dominion of the earth, free access to the throne where our Father is seated, power to deploy angels, power to set the captives free, power to heal, power to raise the dead, and access to the mysteries of heaven. We also have the Holy Spirit to direct, comfort, teach, guide, and warn; and our friend—yes, the Holy Spirit—is a person who is in you, with you, for you, and is your friend.

As Jesus touched my right shoulder and when God broke through hell to get Matthew, that was our day of salvation. The revelation of the fullness of our salvation and all the privileges of the full inheritance became relative as we grew in the understanding of who God is and truly the relationship of who we were to God, Jesus, and the Holy Spirit; the Trinity. As we joined a church that taught us biblical foundations from the Bible and the life of Jesus, it brought understanding of whom our Father was/is and that Daddy wanted us and we were His. I am the apple of my Daddy's eye, a song from one of my favorite singers, Jason Upton. Also, the CD "Trusting Angels" depicts whom our true Daddy is and how we have a relationship with Him.

"For you did not receive the spirit of bondage again to fear, but you received the Spirit of adoption by whom we cry out, 'Abba, Father!'" (Romans 8:15, NKJV).

"To redeem those who were under the law, that we might receive the adoption as sons," (Galatians 4:5, NKJV).

"And because you are sons, God has sent forth the Spirit of His Son into your hearts, crying out, 'Abba, Father!' Therefore you are no longer a slave but a son, and if a son, then an heir of God through Christ," (Galatians 4:6–7, NKJV).

"Having predestined us to adoption as sons by Jesus Christ to Himself, according to the good pleasure of His will, to the praise of the glory of His grace, by which He made us accepted in the Beloved," (Ephesians 1:5–6, NKJV)

"In Him, we have redemption through His blood, the forgiveness of sins, according to the riches of His grace, which He made abound toward us in all wisdom and prudence" (Ephesians 1:7–8, NKJV).

"Having made known to us the mystery of His will, according to His good pleasure, which He purposed in Himself, that in the dispensation of the fullness of the times, He might gather together in one all things in Christ, both which are in heaven and which are on earth—in Him" (Ephesians 1:9–10, KJV). "In Him, also, we have obtained an inheritance, being predestined according to the purpose of Him who works all things according to the counsel of His will that we who first trusted in Christ should be to the praise of His glory" (Ephesians 1: 11–12, NKJV).

"In Him you also *trusted*, after you heard the word of truth, the gospel of your salvation; in whom also, having believed, you were sealed with the Holy Spirit of promise, who is the guarantee of our inheritance until the redemption of the purchased possession, to the praise of His glory" (Ephesians 1: 13–14 NKJV).

These last scriptures give us the fullness of who we are and what we receive as sons and daughters of the Father of the Most High. A summary of what I call key principles follow for those that are known as sons and daughters:

> We have adoption thru Jesus Christ according to the good pleasure of His will
> We are accepted in the Beloved

We have redemption through His blood
We have forgiveness of sins
We have the riches of His grace which He made abundant toward us in all wisdom and prudence
He makes known to us the mystery of His will
That in the dispensation of the fullness of the times, both heaven and in earth, He might gather together in one all things in Christ
That in Him we have obtained an inheritance
That in Him Who works all things according to the counsel of His will
That we who first trusted in Christ should be to the praise of His glory
In Him you also trusted, after you heard the word of truth, the gospel of your salvation
In whom also having believed
You were sealed with the Holy Spirit of promise
He is the guarantee of our inheritance, until the redemption of the purchased possession, that's us
And it's all for the praise of His glory

So do you choose life through Jesus Christ, or death? Do you choose a true inheritance or a false, fallen world with a fallen angel named Lucifer, a.k.a. Satan, who steals, kills, and destroys life, your life? I strongly suggest Jesus, who gives eternal life of love, peace, joy, prosperity, health, power over sickness, and a true inheritance of sons and daughters of the royal kingdom.

"Therefore do not worry, saying, 'What shall we eat?' or 'What shall we drink?' or 'What shall we wear?' For after all these things the Gentiles seek. For your heavenly Father knows that you need all these things. But seek first the *king*dom of God and His righteousness, and all these things shall be added to you" (Matthew 6:31–33, NKJV).

So seek first the *King* (*Melek*). "Endow the king with your justice, O God, the royal son with your righteousness. He will judge your people in righteousness, your afflicted ones with justice. The mountains will bring prosperity to the people, the hills the fruit of righteousness" and His *righteousness* will be added to you, praise the Lord Almighty, (Psalm 72:1–3, NIV).

"God is the King of all the earth," (Psalm 47:7, NKJV).

[Nancy's dialogue]

The hours turned into days and days into weeks, not knowing how long Matthew would be in a coma and if he could function as "normal" again. It was crazy from the beginning. Matthew had everything you could imagine go wrong. He had a high fever. (It was 105 to 110; brain cells start to die around 104.) They had Matthew on an ice blanket; and then they put in an extra large tracheotomy, for they must have thought he would be in a coma for a very long time. They started feeding him through a tube in his nose. My mother called it green lamb chop stuff.

One of the must amazing monitors was the one they screwed into the top of Matthew's head to monitor brain function, swallowing, etc.

We all took shifts sitting at Matthew's side, looking for any movement and anxiously awaiting any encounter with his many doctors. It seemed that there was a separate doctor for all his organs—kidneys, brain, legs, lungs—plus the infectious-disease doctors; a bewildering sea of doctors. Are you wondering about the organ donors? Well, Matthew made it through the first night; but they stayed the next day. Finally, they were released, unsuccessful in harvesting my husband's organs. Thank you, God!

After the third day, the criminals were caught and the hospital was off of the lockdown. A sense of relief was evident in the doctors and nurses. Even in the cafeteria, after breakfast, lunch, and dinner inside the hospital, many hospital employees began to know who we were; and some felt compassion and sadness, sharing in the range of emotions with us about the crime that was committed. Let's talk about some really good food. Oh my goodness. I love fried okra and cornbread. Yeah, it was good Southern cooking, good comfort food; but many times, I had to choke down the meal.

The Kindness of Others

[Nancy's dialogue]

I remember that a lady made a cake every week, sometimes two if she knew out of town people where present, coming to give last good-byes to visit us to bring refreshment of clothes, etc. That cake tasted so good because of the love and compassion the cake lady put into it. Let me advise you to never again hesitate to bake a cake and/or bring a meal. It is so comforting. It's showing love.

The Second Week

[Nancy's dialogue]

Matthew's kidneys started to function improperly. His body was starting to shut down one organ at a time. They were informing or preparing us for his ultimate death. Oh my, did it get scary. Specialized doctors were coming at all different times of the day. I would get a phone call at 4:00 a.m. to come down to ICU for emergency procedures and/or cat scans since I was the legal wife and had to sign and authorize procedures I never even heard of. I tell you, quick decisions became the norm; and I had peace. I was steady and calm in the very midst of this torrential storm. Here's an example of turnaround. Matthew's kidneys had shut down. They put him on kidney dialysis machines—they told us possibly for three weeks. It was only three days; and, yes, it amazed the doctors. Matthew had very high, life-threatening fevers, staff infectious diseases, trouble with breathing—you name it, it happened. Oh not good. It was the hardest week for Matthew. He was a fighter. I remember when a group of our friends drove down from Michigan. It was great to see them and also crushing to share how bad things were. I remember encouraging them all. People came to support us, but we comforted them. This crime touched so many people like a stone being dropped into water and the ripple effect thereafter.

The Third Week

[Nancy's dialogue]

At the end of this week was my birthday; then, the next day was Matthew's. It was very depressing. I felt more alone than any other time. He had up and down days. The focus was keeping the status quo—keeping fevers down, brain swelling down, and increasing movement in arms and legs that did not move. Matthew's muscles were gone. He was wasting away daily. Overall, we all were tried, frustrated, and looking for a miracle. We would meet other families going through tragic times; and then, after a few days or more, they would happily say, "Good luck," and, "Hope things turn around." But it really was a bit discouraging. It left you feeling that there was no end. Routines were established, which helped bring order to chaos, I think. I remember sharing a small, old nurse's dormitory that was connected to the hospital with a long, glass corridor with my parents. I would wake up early, sometimes at 4:00 a.m. or 5:00 a.m., and I would walk through this glass corridor. It seemed to take forever to get to Matthew's room. All the time, I was wondering what trauma would be in store for that day. I felt very alone, almost forgotten. Many years later, the Lord showed me what truly was happening in that long walk every day to Matthew's room. Jesus, adorned in a lengthy robe, kicking out at the floor with each purposeful stride, would be by my side. Heaven's angels filled the expanse of the corridor, accompanying us in flight, light, and song on the daily journey to my husband's room.

The Fourth Week

[Nancy's dialogue]

This week began with Matthew's doctor going out of town for the weekend. Panic struck on the first night. Matthew's brain monitor was showing extreme high numbers, which indicates brain swelling; and worse, high fever added to the fear. All through the night, chaos ensued with nurses trying to keep the fever down; but the brain monitor was very high. Life and death were hanging in the balance. The next morning, the doctor covering for the chief doctor while out of town said, "Let's do a spinal tap." "Oh my God!" I panicked. *This must be serious. The look on the nurse's face tells everything.* I authorized it, and I stayed in the room as the doctor took the largest needle that I have ever seen and pray to God never see again. The doctor said, "Let's do it." All I heard was a pop, which must have been Matthew's spinal cord being punctured; and fluid filled the huge tube.

The doctor said, "Clear. It's all clear," and he looked perplexed.

I looked at a nurse, and she gave me the thumbs-up. *That is good,* I thought to myself.

The chief doctor came back, and he reported that

the monitor was misreading because the skin around the probe grew over it. He started unscrewing the probe out of Matthew's head like unscrewing a soda bottle, Matthew's head twisting with each turn. It made me feel nauseated.

I remember that we would take turns sitting next to Matthew. I would normally hold his right hand, and he would move his fingers involuntary; and it seemed like he would play with my wedding ring. The nurses discounted that because Matthew was in coma's eighth stage. Stage one would be almost normal. He was not aware. One day, he seemed agitated and really playing, almost spinning my ring around and around; then my mom gave me the "you better get something to eat" break look. The anxiousness Matthew was exhibiting playing with my ring moments before stopped as soon as he felt my mom's ring, as if he knew the difference. Telling and trying to convince the nurses this, that Matthew was aware of his environment, was another story. The next day, I was at Matthew's side; and I was moving my thumb back and forth as if playing the thumb game that Matthew would usually cheat at—like at the count one, two, cheat; he would not wait until three. So I played, counting one, two, and his thumb moved on mine. I shouted, "He's in there! He cheated! He's in there!" The nurses took notice and called the doctor. This began the process of bringing Matthew out of the induced, twenty-seven-day coma to life.

WAKING UP

AS RECOUNTED BY MATTHEW

[Matthew's dialogue]

The moment did come when I came out of the coma after twenty-seven days. It began in a quite surreal fashion, as my not-so-accurate eyes tried to focus on the surrounding walls, sterile white but decorated with flashy birthday cards, "Get well" slogans, and "We miss you" banners creating a perplexing border about the room. The birthday cards were depressing. I saw things floating around at the top of my eyes as I scanned the room. I was informed that it was due to the blood that pooled behind my eyes from the great impact velocity of the bullet. They said that eventually, it should clear up. I awoke with my head bandaged, my right arm tied down to a white-sheeted bed, and unable to speak because of a huge hole in my throat. Needles were taped in my arms and chest. I recalled periodically having a tube forced down into my lungs that sucked out all the breath I had to breathe with in order to remove fluids building up in my lungs. It felt like I was being suffocated from the inside. (And they said I wouldn't remember that part because I was comatose.) I couldn't feed myself, walk, or talk. I had a huge, gaping hole in my throat, covered by gauze. My left leg and arm were completely paralyzed, unable to move. I was unable to go to the bathroom as I had all my adult life, much less even be able to time the urgency of bowel movements so someone could get the bed pan under my butt in time before going all over in the bed that I was confined to. Bed sores were appearing in all the places that my skin had prolonged contact to the bed—on my heels, buttocks, elbows, shoulder blades, and hips. See, the nursing staff had to make sure they turned me and rolled me to various lying positions because the muscles that were not totally paralyzed were weakened too much to help and my motor functions were out of order. I did not know how to turn, roll over, sit up, and such—even if my muscles had the strength to do this. Being paralyzed is much more than just having my muscles that are weak; it's all the way to the brain not knowing how to do the movements themselves. I don't even know how I'm supposed to move my left index finger or how to bend my left ankle to this very day, eighteen years later. That's a long time to not remember how to move my left fingers, wrist, or left toes or ankle. It doesn't compute, so to speak.

I can recall wearing a Frankenstein-type boot on my left ankle/foot to keep my foot in a more comfortable, ninety-degree angle while I lay in that bed and to facilitate circulation for all systems that were not operating correctly.

Since there was absolutely no muscle tone in my left ankle or left shoulder, any pressure or pulls on or at those joints were pure pain and agony, even the weight of the bed sheet. So when I first looked at myself, my body weighing in at ninety pounds, legs thin as my arms and not doing what I thought they should be doing, I thought, *My God. What's going on?* I felt some sort of hole that was at the top of my head and not a lot of hair left up there. Obviously, someone had done a fine job of shaving off my hair and wrapped me in what felt like a turban. I looked at my right arm, which had a larger needle taped into it just above my elbow toward the inside. Then, looking down at both arms, I noticed areas where needles had been inserted; removed; and, who knows, probably inserted once again. Some of my veins seemed to have changed from what I recalled them looking like, meaning their color was different; some were larger; some were thinner; some protruded; some were even pretty much flat. A lot of the hair was missing, from taping and retaping I'm sure. I recalled several times throughout the nights of being woken from deep sleep only to have a needle plunged in them, some more painless, some obvious misses by the pain and subjection I endured in the fluorescent pierced dark of many nights, being fed a thick, liquid, green food via a nose tube.

The thought of walking was nonexistent. It was a very interesting thing, thinking back now that my brain seemed to "know" it had been damaged and that my left side's circuitry was faulty because it just knew that my paralyzed parts were paralyzed. It wasn't a matter of discovery for it. The commands in the neurons of my brain that normally functioned for a coordinated movement, such as, "Lift your left arm," were damaged. During the entire time, I was fed a liquid diet, consisting of some kind of green stuff, via my nose. My mother (Nancy's mom) told me after I woke up that she would tell me it tasted like lamb chops; not that I heard her, but that's the positive attitude that gets people through the toughest of times. She, amongst other family members and friends, said that they would speak to me as if I could hear them when they visited me. I did not know details of my very recent past, such as how I got where I was or why I was; but soon enough, people began to fill in the gaps in my memory bank.

I soon learned what a catheter was as I saw beneath my loose, thin gown what was draining my urine for me. Everything was a blur: my life, where I was, what happened—and I really couldn't care less. I was in a state of just existing. What time it was, what day or year, didn't make a difference in the world to me. I couldn't begin to tell you what day of the week or what month it was, much less be confident in the current year. My visual spatial perceptions were so warped that reading an analog clock correctly was hit and miss. I had "left neglect," which, as the name suggests, meant that most everything toward the left side of my field of vision would be neglected, not acknowledged or seen.

The second day, I was forced to sit in a very uncomfortable, cold, vinyl chair, feeling infantile in my attempts to balance my head upon my shoulders and drooling out of the left corner of my mouth because the left side of my face too was paralyzed. My attempt at smiling only worked for the right side of my mouth. I was cold, thin, a wisp of the man I once was. I was using all the strength I could muster with the only arm that functioned to keep myself in that chair very unsuccessfully, for I kept sliding down and off. Even though I had full movement of my right side, it was very weak from the fifty pounds of weight lost and the twenty-seven days of inactivity during the coma. Even the attempt to tie me in to the chair was not successful. As seen in the photo, my left leg was as thin as the armrest of the chair itself. This is when my first attempt at speech began. My first words were, "Hi, bun." I said them to my wife while she was covering the gaping, gauzed-covered hole in my neck. I saw my wife loaded with love and concern. Boy, it was good to see her even though my emotions were flat. I remember my mother came in too, asking me to say, "Hello, Mom." I eventually did say, "Hello, Mom," after a concentrated effort to repeat after someone. My cognitions operated at such a base level that anything more than simple, one-step directions proved too complicated for me to repeat or perform. I saw my brother, and we gave each other thumbs-up with my right hand, obviously with my right thumb. To this day, the thumbs-up gesture brings great emotion to me. I drooled a lot from the left due to its inability to retain saliva. Now that's something somebody my age never thinks about, how to keep the saliva in their mouths. There are medical terms that describe this state of mind after a severe brain injury, but I fondly call it la-la land, a surreal place where all attention is placed on me and getting me better. It took years to get to the place where I could think about others in a balanced love kind of way, as often exhibited by our Savior, Jesus.

After twenty-seven days in a coma, deciding on which rehabilitation center to attend and getting home was our focus and determination. All sorts of literature on rehabilitation centers all over the world were provided for us, but getting back home to Michigan seemed to be the best all-around choice; and by God's grace, there was a good rehab hospital about forty minutes from our home. So the plans began; and after two more weeks of recovery and loads of paperwork, we got discharged from the Georgia hospital.

[Matthew's dialogue]

I remember the fastest plane ride I ever had been on: the medical leer jet that transported us from the Atlanta hospital to the Michigan hospital. I remember that there was Coke on the flight. I don't know why I recall that, but I do. It must have meant something to me at the time. I don't even like pop. There were a couple techs on board who watched my vitals, and my dear wife. Boy, I love her. She's been through so much. Nancy gave up so much of who she is and was for me. Her reward in heaven will certainly be great. I think she'll even have gold bricks in the bathrooms of her heavenly mansion. We arrived at Pontiac airport in one hour and ten minutes by air transport and were transported by med port unit to the Michigan rehabilitation hospital. Thereupon arriving, they immediately quarantined me because they deemed that I had hepatitis C that I must have contracted from the blood infusions in the Georgia emergency room. I lost a lot of blood out on the concrete sidewalk. I never did get my black leather cowboy boots or black leather jacket back because I was told they were covered with my blood and had to be cut off and then thrown away. (I loved those boots and jacket; and today I cannot wear cowboy boots because I wear a leg brace. Bummer.)

Separated Once Again

[Nancy's dialogue]

It was exciting and a little scary traveling on a leer jet for the first time. Matthew seemed to like it, and all I knew was that this was our next step on the long road of recovery. As we arrived to the next step, the rules were a bit different. I was not as free to access the recovery room as I was used to, and I could not stay the night for his adjustment or mine. I remember staying until visitors hour were over, and I did not want to leave Matthew with all the new doctors and nurses. What if they needed me? What if something happened? I was forty minutes away. Oh my God, I was terrified. In Georgia, I was called at all hours of the night. As I rode in the back seat of Pauly and Lucy's (family) car, all I could do was grip the door handle, wanting to get out. We picked up our dog at a friend's house. Boy, it was amazing how good your dog makes you feel. So I was dropped off at our home with my shepherd; and I realized how alone I felt. I was separated again from Matthew. I stood inside my front door for a very long time as all the events of the past seven and a half weeks came flooding into my mind. I was paralyzed. I remember crawling to the phone in the kitchen and calling my parents to please come over and stay with me. It was a long, dark night. The routine began the next morning. I was up early and drove to the rehab hospital to visit Matthew and hang out during some closed sessions every day for two months until LOAs (leaves of absence) were allowed.

On one day during the weekend, Matthew could come home for a very short visit to get acclimated to what home life would be; and I was to get the house handicap accessible. Most of the time, Matthew would just lie on the couch while visitors, family, friends, and neighbors would drop by to say hello.

You ask how I was doing. Well, after four weeks into Matthew's rehab hospital recovery, I was tired and went to the doctor. I had kidney stones. Ouch. Yes, painful, so I rested one day per doctor's orders, but only one day. It is amazing how mind over matter works. I had to see Matthew. He missed me, and I missed him. We were each other's strength. It was exciting to get Matthew finally home after two months in the rehab hospital. Life was full of huge adjustments in every area of our lives. I tried to go back to work for several weeks, but Matthew needed around-the-clock care. Matthew weighed ninety-five pounds; his entire left side of his body was paralyzed; and, cognitively, he was not with it. He was in la-la land. Try to imagine propelling yourself with your right leg and right arm only in a wheel chair. Yeah. Very difficult. Matthew was and is awesome. He had determination, will, heart, and hope that he would have full recovery.

That is the *key* to victory.

[Matthew's dialogue]

The number one question I'm always asked is, "Did you forgive the guys who shot you?"

Wikipedia, the free, Web-based encyclopedia, defines *forgiveness* in the following manner. It is the mental, emotional, and/or spiritual process of ceasing to feel resentment or anger against another person for a perceived offence, difference, or mistake or ceasing to demand punishment or restitution.

Luke's gospel in the Bible speaks of loving your enemies and not judging others. Matthew's gospel likewise declares the importance, i.e., the necessity, of forgiving others for our own welfare. Yes. So, as you can see, great forgiveness on my behalf was quite necessary; and I found it in myself and my wife to not hold the men responsible for what they did to me. We hold satan accountable for the men's actions, and our Father in heaven will dole out the verdicts at the end of the ages.

I see *adaptation* as a process whereby changes are made to better suit a person's environment or habitat. After some thought into this, my belief is that a person must be humble in character for successful adaptation to occur. A humble person is more apt to embrace change than fight against it. In fact, if one wants help, i.e., grace from God in any situation, they must not be proud. The Apostle James refers to God resisting the proud but giving grace to the humble in his epistle (James 4:6, NKJV). If I ever needed grace to get through a situation, it definitely was this situation. I could have chosen to live in the questions of, "Why did this happen to me?" or, "Why would a loving God let something so terrible happen on His watch?" I think that one of the aspects in answering these questions was that God revealed something to me early on in my injury. That was that it really had nothing to do with God. It had everything to do with choices that were made by men who were following an evil voice in their lives. We know there are basically two realms in existence; and we see them played out in books, plays, movies, television shows, and more. I'm talking about good versus evil. We know that all satan desires is to steal kill and destroy (John 10:10, NKJV) and he uses mankind all that he can. That's the evil realm. satan roams around, seeking whom he may devour—again, the evil realm (1 Peter 5:8, NKJV). Well, it seems that satan tried to devour me using men he could influence to do evil deeds. Notice that I did not say that satan used evil men. The men in and of themselves were children of God, just like any other person on this planet. They just did not know they were created by and for a loving Father. Instead, they filled their lives with wrath, performing evil deeds for the father of lies. Just one touch by our heavenly Father and their lives would not be being wasted and used for evil. Just one choice on their behalf to follow the Lamb of God and fulfillment and destiny would have lay before them instead of prison doors. That's all it takes, just one touch by our Father in heaven, one choice for the Lamb of God. Were it not for this revelation early on, surely I would have consumed my life with the "Why me?" questions. So I thank the Father for His generous gift of wisdom. So that's why the process of adaptation was something I could choose to undertake valiantly and not with great anger for what I had lost. I saw myself as victorious from day one. Please don't misunderstand me as meaning that frustration and anger never entered, for they did; and I'm sorry to say that besides at myself, my dear wife probably took the next brunt of my frustrations in the early days of adapting to being paralyzed.

[Matthew's dialogue]

I recently heard a magnificent teaching by John Paul Jackson entitled "The Two Trees" to further emphasize this point of good versus evil on the two trees that were in the Garden of Eden; the tree of life and the tree of knowledge of good and evil. What so impacted me was the simplicity of the presumption of the teaching. Simply said, it was that all choices either come from the tree of life or the tree of knowledge. Jesus is the tree of life; hence, all choices in or through Him result in life, as opposed to all the choices from the tree of knowledge, which will produce death. If God isn't giving you the answer or providing the choice, then it's satan's realm that is. As we can see, death was the result from the gunmen's choices.

REHABILITATION
MATTHEW'S DIALOGUE

[Matthew's dialogue]

After being shot and stripped of everything I deemed valuable and important in my life—job, finances, being the head of the household, husbandly duties, masculinity, and all-around fixer and jack of all trades—little did I know that I was being set up for success in the kingdom of God. When you realize that true success has a lot to do with the forging of your character then success is redefined. Even if you do not know God, these still apply to your life. Peter writes in his second epistle in chapter one verses 5–7 that we are to, with all diligence, add virtue to our faith, and to knowledge self-control, to self-control perseverance, to perseverance godliness, to godliness brotherly kindness, and to brotherly kindness love. He goes on to say that if these seven things are yours and abound, we will never be barren or unfruitful in the knowledge of our Lord, Jesus Christ. By default, I learned that it's a matter of redefinition of my thoughts to God's thoughts or realignment to His, which I never considered before. I think that that's when the full acceptance that God loves me just as I am became a deeply held belief in my heart. As a matter of fact, that's what I rely on today when rejections and stigmas are cast upon me; I turn my heart toward God to receive His affirming or correcting nod. "How do you receive a nod from God?" you might ask. It's as easy as listening for or feeling that small, good voice or nudge from the inside. Some call it your conscience; but if you're hurting on the inside, you'll instead hear satan telling you that you deserved it, telling you that you're no good. Listen. Satan will do anything to disrupt your ability to believe you can commune with the living God. He (satan) tried to use that "you're not doing something right" attack (attacking my righteousness) early on as I stood (and still stand today), contending for my healing until I came to know deep, experientially, in my heart that it's not my righteousness anyway; it's God's righteousness that I have because I have His Son, Jesus, and the Holy Ghost. He (satan) so desires to split up all families—natural and spiritual—and he loves using brother against brother, sister against sister, siblings against parents, and even parents against siblings. God has placed me in a specific time and place for a specific purpose. The shooting did not derail me from my life's destiny. You may think that life has derailed you because of a decision you made or a decision that was made for you. For me, the shooting in fact put me on God's rails of destiny.

When a person becomes defeated, unable to fend for themselves, he or she must see victory in his or her life or they will stay a defeated victim in all they do. Me, I saw challenge ahead of me. I had beaten the odds and predictions already, for I did survive and I was learning how to speak and think via some fine speech and cognitive therapists; and I was being strengthened by recreational therapists in the pool for the momentous day that my physical therapists would attempt to get me standing or at least able to transfer from wheelchair to toilet or shower chair with great assistance. And occupational therapists were trying to assist my upper body mobility and for I was being told (not directly, not right away anyway) by various medical professionals that walking was not something I would do again. God bless them for all their good deeds on my behalf though, before I reached the infamous one-year post-injury plateau. So I better get all the gains I could before that one-year anniversary date. I recall the unbearable pain of something so light and thin as the bed sheet lying atop my left foot, bending my toes backward and my ankle in all sorts of ways because all muscle tone and motor coordination had disappeared in an instant. The pain in my left shoulder was excruciating, for there was not enough muscle tone to hold it in the socket; so the RN's would prop a pillow beneath my left elbow to prop it up and support it in the socket. Feeding myself was quite the feat. Even though my right side had not been paralyzed, it was affected by lack of strength and diminished coordination. I remember the first time I tried to take a spoon to my mouth. The first part of the challenge was getting the food to be on the spork (a spoon-fork combination). Just getting the food onto that contraption that was made to enhance the ease with which to secure the morsel seemed ridiculous, especially when the morsel of food outran the sides of the plate as I tried and tried again to scoop/stab the food. I even was supplied with special, high-sided plates that quarantined the food into small areas. Even the plate had a bottom side that made the plate stay put on the tray left over my lap in the hospital bed. The times when I did get food secured on the spork, I had to get it into my mouth, which was another feat unto itself. Learning to chew and swallow was worked on to. Remember, I was on a green liquid diet for just shy of a month and I didn't need to chew nor swallow that stuff. It went straight down my throat and into my stomach. Sitting up was impossible. Even rolling over didn't make any sense. I didn't even remember how to begin either of those movements. I had to buzz a nurse to do it for me, but I would just usually wait for them to check in on me and then do the repositioning. Sometimes in the process of repositioning, my left arm would be lost behind my back. Later, when I regained some strength and coordination and just plain ole relearned what to do, I had to hold my left arm with my right before I began to move at all or I would lose it. "How does one lose their own arm?" you might ask. There is a fancy word, *proprioception*, that means that your brain basically knows where your body parts are all the time. With me, if I can't see it with my eyes, then I can't tell where it is. That's why it's possible for me to roll over on my own arm, the left, only to dislocate my shoulder or sprain a wrist or finger. Then I embarrassingly became aware that I could not control my bowels. By the time I could say I needed the bed pan, it was too late; and green slime was all over the place in the bed sheets. And you know, the funny thing about it is that I couldn't care less that I, a grown man, just messed the bed. Periodically, I would wear what I fondly termed my "Frankenstein boots," an apparatus they would put on my ankle/foot and pressurize to keep my foot in place. I also can recall some very chilly sleep times when they would be placing me in an ice bath to reduce my 105-plus-degree temperatures. Of course, I just recall the extreme discomfort and not the specifics of what they were doing to me until being told of the various treatments given to me early on once out of the coma. That's how much things didn't matter as I lived in my la-la land. My surreal residence in this faraway cerebral country probably lasted a couple years. Even after a year of being shuttled from home to hospital for outpatient therapy, my cognition was off. Once discharged from the inpatient rehab hospital after an approximately two-month stay, I was released to go home only to begin attendance in an all-day drop-off, outpatient, six-month therapy program. In order to help me not get lost during the day at the rehab hospital, my schedule was taped to the clear plastic lap table attached to my wheelchair. I think that part of the speech cognitive therapists' job was watching me to see if I could first navigate the halls of the hospital and then to do it so I could arrive on time at the various therapeutic modalities. In fact, every one of the therapists took note of my arrival times. It was kind of like getting spied on anonymously while taking a test over and over. I remember as my cognitions began to gel and I started living in this world that constant overseeing began to make me feel slighted. I mean, I was an adult, you know. The day would begin with my wife helping me out of bed and into my wheelchair parked by the bed; then on into the bathroom to transfer me (lift me) to the toilet. Actually, as my wife so fondly reminded me upon waking in the morning, I had to pee even before getting out of bed, so she usually would go to the bathroom to retrieve my plastic urinal and bring it back to me, all the while hoping I was going to be able to hold my urine long enough for her return, help me get situated so I could go in the plastic container which was often a trick in and of itself, especially if I was cold, if you know what I mean; and using only one hand to hold urinal and aim my penis in it too. Often, in the middle of the night, the same pattern might occur. I remember one instance when I was sitting on the toilet and I fell off to the one side and got stuck, or better yet wedged, between the toilet and the wall because my body wasn't strong enough to hold itself upright while on the toilet. If a shower was necessary, she would lift me onto the wide shower chair in the stand-up shower and help me wash with a handheld shower head. When done, she would lift me out back onto the wheelchair, sometimes still wet because, remember, even though I lost over fifty pounds from being in the coma for twenty-seven days, I still weighed enough (ninety pounds) to make it hard for her to solely lift a wet noodle of a person. Then she had to dress me, feed me, and then wheel me out of our ranch-style home, down the wooden ramp (that my brother-in-law, Pauly, made) put in place as an accommodation to my sudden circumstances, transfer me in to the car, buckle me up, break down the wheelchair and put it in the trunk, and drive me to the outpatient rehab center, transfer (lift) me from the car back into the wheelchair, and push me into the center for the day—my wife stayed with me at the outpatient rehab—to learn new techniques for life. A funny thing would happen pretty infrequently—but, nonetheless, it would happen from time to time; and that was that I would fall, be dropped solid to the ground on my butt, only to break out in gut-wrenching laughter for what else was there to do. I could not stand myself back up or even help her get me back up, so I sat on the ground or lay in a panicky laugh. Usually, something like my left elbow or knuckles on my left hand got skinned and bloody because I could not protect my left arm very well. I soon learned that after numerous falls over the years, my instinctual drives began to kick in, and I would tuck in my left arm when I fell, holding it in with my right in an attempt to protect it. I saw couples become singles left and right; sometimes the injured leaving the spouse because the injured couldn't deal with themselves and sometimes the uninjured leaving the injured one because, well, you can probably guess why the uninjured often left the injured and ended the marriage figuring, "That wasn't part of the deal when I said I do!" But Nancy was always with me in therapies and through the long road ahead with love and hope in her eyes.

The various therapeutic modalities—physical and cognitive—were painful. I'm not sure how to explain in words what cognitively painful actually means except imagine yourself staring at and thinking about nothing else but moving your index finger, or any finger for that matter, and you try so hard to move it that you get out of breath or forget about breathing all together, your face turns red and brow becomes moist with perspiration, and the therapist has to remind you to breath and says, "Okay. That's enough for now. We'll do more later on." It's that sort of pain. The physical pain is probably easier to understand because most people have had sore muscles or tendons at one point in their life, so they have a construct to understand by. The experience created what I call a construct, a set of definitions based on experiences that one can thereby understand. Paralysis and cognitive pain most do not have a construct to understand. I'm doing my best to convey. Cognitive pain also entails weariness. My brain became weary in repeated attempts to move a body part that didn't move or learn something lost due to brain injury. Because my unaffected side was my right arm and leg, that meant I had to figure out how to push/pull my wheelchair in a straight line when the simple physics of the situation meant that I should go around in a circle counterclockwise. Plus, I was left-hand dominant; therefore, a complete retraining had to be done. So, between therapy appointments, I'd practice writing the alphabet with my right hand. At the very beginning, I practiced just remembering the alphabet and where the sun rose and set in the sky (e.g., the sun rises in the east and sets in the west). I was taught by the cognitive therapists to use various tricks for increasing my ability to remember a lot of things. My short-term memory was terrible.

There were chunks of long-term memory missing too; but the interesting aspect is that when someone spoke of an event I had forgotten, it triggered the memory and then I could access that memory/event in my memory bank. Sounds a bit computerized to me as I write about it; but, nonetheless, that's how it worked for me. You should experience opening up your calendar, seeing your own handwritten entries with appointments crossed out, and yet not having the foggiest idea that they ever occurred. It's a little unsettling and definitely weird. So I had physical therapists assist me in strengthening aspects relating to my core and lower extremities; occupational therapists who worked on my upper extremities, including the adaptation to feeding, cooking, and general hygiene; recreational therapists who tried to bring some recreation, some fun, back into my now-disabled body, adapting to life, and also incorporated strengthening too. Speech therapists, as the name suggests, worked with me on my speech; and the cognitive therapists worked on the exercising of higher-level decision-making processes. Hollywood is making television shows and movies about this type of stuff, and I got to and get to live and experience it first-hand—not to mention the effects on my wife and the necessary adaptations she's had to make. Its eighteen years post-injury now; and, yes, I'm typing this book one-handed, with my right hand. A curious aspect of my injury is that it is supposed to be static in its medical nature, but it is definitely dynamic in the adaptive aspects. Adaptation is a continual, lifelong process in a world devised and developed for people with two arms and two legs who can walk, work, and play; so, unless

I die (for good this time) right now, I will always be encountering situations that I have to conquer by doing them differently than most people. Of course, if you're a Christian, then you are already different than a lot of people, for you have the living Son of God inside and the Holy Ghost to help guide you.

[Matthew's dialogue]

When my long-awaited one-year anniversary came and went, the rehab center made the decision that my recovery was complete. This was very confusing to me and my wife. Here are some of the facts of my rehabilitated condition upon discharge. I was using a wheelchair most of the time. I could walk *very* short distances with a brace/orthotic on my left knee/ankle/foot, using a cane or modified ski pole for balance and to help bear the weight. I was legally driving once again because my seizures were successfully being controlled by meds and I had passed the driving examinations in rehab. My left arm was pretty much nonfunctional. When I fell out of the wheelchair or fell to the ground at any time, I was stuck there until someone came to lift me up to the wheelchair or cane. Nancy and I both said to ourselves, *You got to be kidding me. Surely there's more*, referring to my recovery. It was really frowned upon by my current physicians because anything outside of their conventional therapeutic modalities was just unacceptable—even to the point that they would no longer want to be professionally considered as my primary MD, literally walked away as I sat in the wheelchair, watching their backsides. Imagine my thoughts, me watching them walk away from me still seated in my wheelchair vantage point. Every ounce, every cell, every emotion of my wife and me was yelling out, "There's got to be more!"

[Nancy's dialogue]

So, on to South Florida we went, with every expectation, every hope, and every bet, so to speak, on the line. Even a fund was set up whereby business associates could help fund this expensive, all-or-nothing endeavor. We visited for two weeks for intensive rehab of what turned out to be many visits at a place called the Upledger Institute. The rehab included intensive deep skeletal massage therapy that attempted to teach the body to crawl and roll over using muscles that were paralyzed and many more very intensive therapies that did further his rehabilitation. I can't help but think that if we would have listened to the doctors' advice we would have missed months, maybe years of advancement in Matthew's recovery. Also, the weather was so beautiful, sunny, happy, warm, and easy to be mobile. Matthew's parents owned a town home a scant four miles from the rehab facility. Talk about a God setup. As we look back, we see God's hand all over many things, not just pulling

Matthew from the confines of hell. Then we noticed how Matthew moved better in the humidity and heat compared to the dryer, colder climate of Michigan. There is nothing like pushing a wheelchair through a couple feet of snow to make one reconsider where they live. So up for sale our house went, and we moved to central Florida (Gainesville) in the summer of '94.

[Matthew's dialogue]

We moved to Florida, away from family, friends, doctors, and all the support teams we had. It was just Nancy and me (Matthew) and our dog.

There I was, newly arrived with my wife in the sunny state of Florida, making great attempts to walk with my dog, having to constantly remind him to heel; otherwise, I would end up face down on the hard, asphalt, paved road. Being fresh out of the wheelchair and able to walk very short distances made this excursion with our dog quite dangerous for me physically, but I recall really wanting to do something on my own that resembled what I could do before being injured; so off I went into the streets in our new neighborhood (really only the street immediately in front of our home). There, a neighbor was walking his dog. He came up along my side, my left side I think because my dog leash was in my right hand; and I looked over and up at him, for he was taller than me, and I spoke these words: "Hey, where's a good church around here?" No sooner had I opened my mouth than those words came flying out—"Hey, where's a good church around here?"—like I rehearsed them for that very moment in time. Well, needless to say, it floored me what came out of my mouth. We were in no way looking for a church. We had just moved in, leaving Michigan where we grew up and lived for the first twenty-eight years of our lives, left all our family and friends to come to a distant state like Florida all because I felt better in the warmer, humid climate; and we had also determined that I should attempt to retrain myself for the work world (at the local university). We still had boxes not yet unpacked we were so fresh in our new home. My wife freaked out when I told her what came out my mouth, those few words of, "Hey, where's a good church around here?" to our neighbor. She replied, "What? We're not looking for a church." I did not know what came over me to say such a thing; and even better yet, as we would soon find out, I asked this of a fellow that was a big-time worshipper of the Lord, radical some would say at that time, an ardent church attendee. Well, anyway, he did make a church recommendation; and it was by my love for the violin that actually got us to one church service. His son was playing in a grand Easter program at the local university's theater, so we attended. This man and his family began praying for us and living out Matthew 22:37–40 (NKJV): "Jesus said to him, '*You shall love the LORD your*

God with all your heart, with all your soul, and with your entire mind. This is *the* first and great commandment. And *the* second *is* like it: *'You shall love your neighbor as yourself.'* On these two commandments hang all the Law and the Prophets." It was there that after the pastor made an altar call for those to give their lives to the Lord and get saved that we, Nancy and I, looked at each other and knew in our hearts that we were already saved by what happened to us both back in March of 1992 and needed not leave the balcony we were seated in to go front toward the altar. (Jesus does say in Matthew 10:32 (NKJV), "Therefore whoever confesses Me before men, him I will also confess before My Father who is in heaven.") So I'm not abdicating one way or another to come to the Lord; I'm just telling you about how our salvation occurred. Our church attendance began sporadically. The worship that always occurred first in the church services brought forth the deep, intense pain we were carrying in our hearts; so we decided that, instead of allowing the Lord to minister and heal us, we would time our arrival when worship was finished and the pastor was beginning to deliver his message to the congregation. And, yes, we sat in the back. It does not matter where you sit; God is everywhere.

BACK TO SCHOOL

[Matthew's dialogue]

Upon reaching Florida, both Nancy and I were enrolled in the local university to get a new skill set for our changed lives. I, with the Americans with Disabilities Act (ADA) on my side, was enabled to enter into a graduate program in rehabilitation counseling. It seemed logical at the time to learn how to help others with acquired disabilities such as myself. The ADA allowed for special test-taking parameters such as extended time periods, distraction-free environments (distractibility and slower processing speeds are common problems after head injuries) and an extension to complete the MHS program overall. Simultaneously, Nancy enrolled in the same university's undergraduate program in speech pathology, for what better area of expertise for her to major in since she had hands-on experience with me, her own husband. My seizures were hit and miss; and when I had one, I had to refrain from driving for a year, so she was driving us both to the campus for our classes and various studies. It is a miracle in and of itself that our class schedules pretty much coincided with each other's. Even though my studies and subsequent graduation resulted in a master's degree that I cannot implement today because of my inability to re-enter the workforce, I do not regard any time or money at the university ill spent. The mental cognitions necessary to attend school at the graduate level for me honed my executive functions beyond that which they would of ever been had I not had those challenges following my brain injury. It was physically challenging too, for the campus was large, doors were big, and book bags were heavy. With all of that, coupled with me walking with a cane in my right hand, things got difficult and frustrating a lot of the time. However, I had some great classmates step outside of themselves and lend helping hands when I needed them the most. My wife graduated from her program with honors, praise the Lord. I received an achievement and leadership award during my studies and graduated successfully too. Then the day came to return to work. I secured a job at a local rehabilitation counseling workplace that specialized in treating people with TBI, traumatic brain injuries. It seemed a good fit for me since I was managing mine quite well by most accounts and opinions. My wife became employed at the same time at the same business too. Thanks to the ADA, the business I was employed at allowed half-day work schedules, working just a few days a week. I went through a series of reducing my work days and work hours per day, trying to find that which I was capable of being successful at. Eventually, the reductions led to my dismissal entirely from the job due to the cognitive errors I made unknowingly during my work periods. Nancy was also let go of her work at approximately the same time. For her, working with people who had sustained head injuries proved interesting in that it enabled her firsthand knowledge of my deficits. That proved challenging for her because she was dealing with folks with deficits from head injuries at work for eight hours and then returned home to her husband after work hours and was confronted with the same type of deficits. Back to me losing my job. Work in the real world was something I just couldn't keep up with after sustaining my head injury. To this day, I'm very glad that I made a 100 percent attempt at getting back in the work force, regardless of the negative outcome. I read a quote from H. Jackson Brown, Jr. that said, "Life doesn't require that we be the best, only that we try our best." That's all I can say that I did. I tried my best to reintegrate into society.

So my question to you is, What is holding you back from doing what is deep in your heart? What is holding you back from starting that new company or living out the dream that you have? What is holding you back from trying?

Matthew chapter 19, verse 26 (NKJV) says, "But with God all things are possible." Don't let fear have its way in your life and shut down your God-given creativity to *try*. See 2 Timothy 1:7 (NKJV): "For God has not given us a spirit of fear, but of power and of love and of a sound mind." Fear is a beast in its ability to conquer, to steal futures, and to kill the life from your present. It will destroy your dreams. It will destroy your desires. Fear will keep you in a box, as will doubt. Sounds similar to the Bible verse describing satan's activities, doesn't it? John 10:10 (NKJV): "The thief comes not, but for to steal, and to kill, and to destroy: I have come that they might have life and that they might have it more abundantly." That is because fear is not from God. Satan has used that paralyzing emotion of fear and doubt on us humans ever since God created us. He (satan) used doubt on Eve in the garden, saying, "Has God indeed said?" God motivates us through His love, for He is love. satan is everything opposite of love. Opposite is a form of the word *opposing,* and that is exactly what satan does day and night before God. He accuses and opposes us here on Earth, trying to cast doubt upon us as often as he can. I myself surely prefer to align myself with the Creator of the entire universe, who was for me. He is for the success of all of us here on this planet. Choose Him and choose life.

When writing this, I was reminded of how scary it was for me to take that first step with my right foot, having to just briefly hold all my weight on my oh-so-weak left leg. The doubt that crept in looking at the daunting task of learning to walk all over again was immense. Having to learn how to walk again is not something a person figures on doing as an adult or prepares themselves for just in case it should happen. No. Walking is supposed to be learned only once in a lifetime. I recall my therapist wrapping a thick belt around my waist and helping support me in my repeated attempts to just slide my right foot forward, much less lift my right foot entirely off of the ground, which, as you know, is what must be done to walk properly. I trusted her that if I was to fall, she would do everything in her power to help me, to prevent me from being harmed. Learning to walk caused a lot of fear and distress in me; but as I tried, I knew that she would be there. Even though I wanted to be free from that wheelchair, it provided me with a sense of security. In all honesty, there was a psychological aspect to the extra attention being in a wheelchair got me that made me feel good, that made me feel more important, valued even. Although this was a dysfunctional psychological mindset, it did creep in at times. Who's kidding who? We all like a little attention now and then. So, with the belt firm about my waist and a hand (or two) on my hips, I knew that I was not alone in this endeavor. This is such a great prophetic parallel to the Holy Spirit and the Lord. He said that He will never leave us or forsake us. That's a comforting thought. Deuteronomy 31:6 (NKJV), says, "Be strong and of good courage, do not fear nor be afraid of them; for the LORD your God, He is the One who goes with you. He will not leave you nor forsake you." He's that close. Jeremiah 23:23 (NKJV) says, "'Am I a God near at hand,' says the LORD, 'And not a God afar off.'" He's there to pick us back up when we do fall. But like a good daddy here on Earth, it makes Him proud as a parent to see us trying and makes Him the happiest when we trust Him enough to just go for it, knowing that He will be there for us.

LIFE TRANSITIONS

[Matthew's dialogue]

After realizing that re-entry in to the world of work was not something that I was going to be successful at, we shifted our focus to what I like to call the maintenance stage of my injury. Basically, any organized rehabilitation efforts ceased and the medical recommendations shifted to keeping as active as possible to delay musculoskeletal deterioration, which is just a fancy way of saying going downhill physically and cognitively as I aged. After five years of living in Gainesville, Florida, my parents told us that they were interested in buying a second home in our area someplace. Nancy and I helped them by looking in our free time out thirty minutes east of Gainesville in a small town named Melrose, situated on a big lake. My parents' preference was to be on water. Their main home in Michigan is on water to this day. Interestingly enough, as we looked for a home for them out in the Melrose area, Nancy and I felt a stirring inside of us that maybe we should be the ones looking for a home. As we looked, we came upon a home that was appealing to us; and simultaneously, a home that was appealing to my parents was found both on the same lake in the same town of Melrose. So, after five and a half years in Gainesville, we left the security we had built up in that church through good friendships and the church itself and moved to Melrose, Florida. At first, we drove back and forth to Gainesville for every church service at least twice per week. Then that tapered off to just Sundays; and what the Lord was doing was forcing us to grow up in Him, to mature in Him due to the circumstances we found ourselves in. We found ourselves building a foundation of wisdom from on high that would not have been possible if we had stayed in the secure nest of Gainesville and the church. It was delightful to see my mom and dad find a little, local church in Melrose that they attended when over wintering in Florida, escaping the cold of Michigan. A deeper relationship with Father God was fostered on their behalf in this little congregation. Each began and continues to see Daddy God for Whom He really is: a lover of all His kids, regardless of age, race, or situation.

One of the pastors from the Gainesville church was sent out to south Florida to plant a sister church in Boca Raton, and Nancy and I had a strong inkling that we were to go south to help in the planting. However, we did not go south immediately but waited on the Lord's timing for us to make such a move. The time came two and a half years after moving to Melrose that we felt that He said go, so we did. We didn't even wait for our home in Melrose to sell first. We were obedient to His command promptly. How we got a mortgage to buy a home down in Boca while retaining the Melrose home is a mystery to me. It didn't come without a fight though; but it did come, and we moved south. Now, in Boca, we had our spiritual senses; our spiritual man/woman expanded in supernatural ways. The ways of the enemy were revealed to us in greater supernatural ways too. A sense of freedom from religiosity incubated and began emerging in our relationship with the Father, Son, and Holy Spirit. We made deep and lasting relationships that were necessary to further our more accurate view of our Daddy and His heart. One special relationship brought to view for us that healing was for today. It opened our eyes to the revelation of healing. Simply put, our Daddy wants all His children healed. He healed in the past. Just look at the Bible, resplendent with examples of His healing power. He can heal today. And He will heal tomorrow, for He is the same yesterday, today, and tomorrow (Hebrews 13:8, NKJV). Our spiritual senses continued to be expanded and honed; but, most importantly, our love for Daddy grew hotter and hotter as we experienced various ministry streams while we lived in the Boca Raton area, participating in leader schools, conferences, and the like—all which expanded our spiritual wineskins (often giving us new wineskins to hold the new wine). Wineskins are representative of our spiritual containers, whereby Holy Spirit resides and deposits His anointing. The various ministry streams often were located outside of the US.

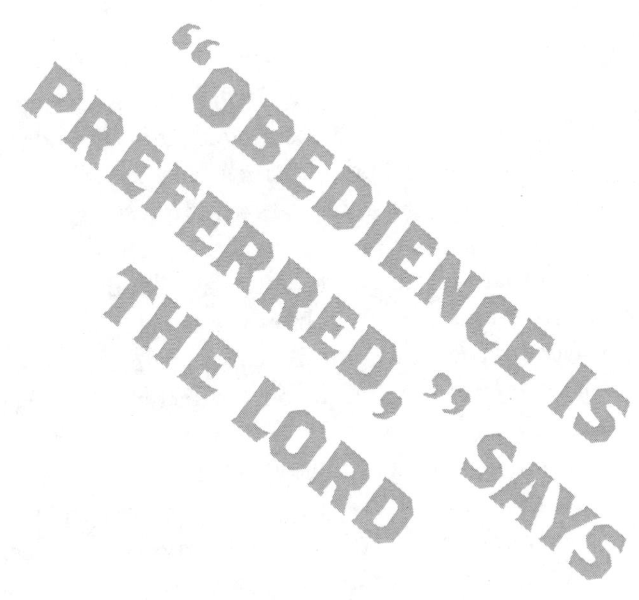

As our paths have proved, obedience is preferred by the Lord, as evidenced by the lasting fruit in our lives. When we heard the Lord say to put our home up for sale, we encountered great resistance in the form of church leaders whom we respected and good friends all advising that we were not hearing from the Lord or that our hearing was faulty. There is wisdom in a multitude of counselors as written in the Bible, yet sometimes you might be the only one hearing Him correctly. Then you, like us, need the courage that only God provides to follow His dictates, His plan. We saw those disagreeing with many of our plans and moves coming back to us in agreement with our earlier moves and some needing to repent for judgments made on their behalf as the fruit grew (when they saw our successes in the Lord). Our point in all of this is that it's best to be obedient immediately to the Word of the Lord in your life, regardless of the circumstances surrounding you. You may not get everything right (as we didn't get everything right); but at least you, like us, will be stepping out and God would rather have you stepping out in action on what you believe is His plan for your life rather than stay anchored in the bay. Not much character growth can occur without the tribulations that the waves outside of the protective bay create, and we know that God is interested in our character being shaped and molded to His. We spent a month on location in Toronto at a leader's school that then led to our first ministry trip abroad—three different countries over three weeks' time. We also celebrated our sixteenth wedding anniversary in Paris while over there. *Oui* is French for "yes" and is pronounced "we" with an exclamation in English. We officially formed our ministry, Seeds of Love; and we began ministering in various places as invited. During this period, we were feeling that familiar stirring that the Lord was up to something; so while on our trip abroad, we were looking at property, investigating monetary exchange rates—we were open to whatever the Lord might be brewing up because we knew by patterns in our own lives past how He begins a work and how transitional phases begin.

DO WHAT?

We heard the Lord say to put our home up for sale, but with no destination mentioned; and, as you might expect, we encountered great resistance again in the form of church leaders that we respected and good friends all advising that we were not hearing from the Lord. There is wisdom in a multitude of counselors, as written in the Bible; yet, sometimes, you might be the only one hearing Him correctly. Then you, like us, need the courage that only God provides to follow His dictates, His plan. For three weeks, we were seeking Him, asking Him, fasting, and praying for where we were supposed to move to. It's quite unnerving to hear Him tell you to put your home up for sale but not tell you where you are going. The silence was deafening on behalf of our Father in Heaven. The only voices were those of people disagreeing with us. At the end of week three, finally, we heard and felt Him say, "By the end of this week you'll know." It was a great comfort to us when we got a call from a friend intercessor, saying, "I don't know what you guys are doing, but by the end of this week, you'll have your answer." So the Lord says to my wife, "Go get a map." She grabbed our Florida map from the car. Then the Lord says to me, "Go get a bigger map." So she grabs the United States map. The Holy Spirit then had my wife to point to Atlanta, Georgia. We freaked, for that was the city of my shooting in the very first place. So great. We don't know anyone there, no family, nothing; all we knew was that my wife noticed a big lake just outside of Atlanta. So we said, "Well okay, Lord." "Obedience is preferred," says the Lord as our paths have proved by the lasting fruit in our lives thus far. In this transaction, the Lord didn't allow us to go search out the land until we had the nonrefundable earnest money in hand for the sale of this Boca Raton home. God's timing was perfect in that the real estate market was hot and at its peak. Again we saw those disagreeing with many of our plans and moves coming back to us in agreement with our earlier moves and some needing to repent for judgments made on their behalf. My point in all of this is that it's best to be obedient immediately to the Word of the Lord in your life, regardless of the circumstances surrounding you. Here is an example of one of many confirmations we received. Nancy had a vision that we had three contracts on our kitchen table and the Lord was saying, "Pick one." And that is exactly what came to pass. How we knew it was not the devil speaking in our ears was due to our intimate relationship with the Father, Son, and Holy Spirit; and that is the key to hearing rightly from Him—loving Him firstly, trusting Him, and having the intimacy with Him to know His voice. Jesus says, "My sheep know My Voice."

The reason the naysayers were unable to derail our plans and subsequent move is due to the intimate relationship with God our Daddy, meaning we knew that we knew that we knew what He told us to do. It's the intimate relationship with the Trinity: Father, Son, and Holy Ghost, that enables you to follow Him. It's the same relationship that makes you *un*-offendable by others—even if they are making decisions for you and about you. Believe me. All the times we've been overlooked and passed over because of my handicapped appearances, we've got a lot of reasons to pick up many ugly offenses if not for the saving grace of our relationship with Daddy. This is the only way a person can travel through life not being offended as Jesus asks us. I've had many what I term "Jesse and David" experiences, meaning I was looked upon from the exterior until a Samuel, a prophet of the Lord, shows up that sees the inside of me setting the record straight. First Samuel 16:7 (NKJV): "But the LORD said to Samuel, 'Do not look at his appearance or at his physical stature, because I have refused him. For *the LORD does* not *see* as man sees; for man looks at the outward appearance, but the LORD looks at the heart.'" We always must be certain to look at what Jesus looks at, and that is the inside of the proverbial teacup. The heart of the man is what is of utmost importance to God. The sooner we learn that the most important part of our journey is continually advancing in our ability to love God in Truth and then others, the sooner the church will advance and keep the ground it's taken.

Jealousy, others' insecurity, and good intentions will often hinder you in your advancements if you let them. They will become walls to God's will for your life. Those things are not from God.

Georgia proved to be a place of further foundation-building and maturing. Our foundations were dug deep and strong by the years in Georgia. What was amazing was with each move, the Lord was positioning us for another level of advancement. One aspect was meeting the producer of *The 700 Club* (a television station in the Christian world) who interviewed us about our amazing testimony. Over 650 salvations called in on the first airing of our testimony, praise to God. The segment has aired many times since then. Many important relationships were developed and are still very important to us today. So here we are, three years living in sunny Georgia, and a pastor friend said, "Why don't you go rent a cabin in the mountains and write your testimony book?" We thought about it. We attended a

Harvest Fest and Worship and Warfare conference in South Carolina. Believe it or not, there was a vendor there exhibiting cabins and land by the mountains; and the Lord said, "Go put your feet on the land." So, with curious imagination, we set out on the adventure God had for us. With God, your journey is always exciting and adventurous. We arrived in Moravian Falls in a subdivision called West Meadows. There, we looked around at the beautiful lots for sale and the amenities that included a small vineyard, club house, garden area, and many walking trails. We both heard God say, "This is not it." We both thought, *Okay, next.* We arrived at a wonderful lodge to sleep for the night. The sweet owners let us share our/God's vision, and they just smiled and nodded—like this wasn't the first time hearing plans such as these from folks such as ourselves. They informed us of a going away party at their lodge that night and invited us for the festivities. Did we have any other choice? We had to stay there, for we were kindly abandoned by the realtor. That night, the Lord spoke very clearly to me (Nancy) and said, "I send one family out and bring one family in." I looked around and thought, *Us? Bring us in as the new family in this community?* At the end of the party, meeting various people that could be our future family, we met a wonderful, newly married couple that became very dear and precious to us. The man said that he was a new realtor and had ten acres with a log cabin on it for sale and asked if we'd like to see it. We both perked up and said that, yes, we would love to see it. Going to sleep that night was difficult because the party did not end until

2:00 a.m. with worship of praises and drums just below our upstairs bedroom, and we were exhilarated with the prospect of what God might be doing in our midst now. The next morning, we drove to our new acquaintance's cabin for a wonderful, home-cooked breakfast, after which we all headed out for our showing of the cabin for sale. Funny though. We only drove down the mountain and then up the next road and turned left. As we drove up the long driveway and saw a glimpse of the cabin home, we both knew that that was it, our new place of positioning by the Lord.

We drove back to our home in Georgia after the showing; and upon arrival back home, the Lord said for us to "leave this country." And He said it with great urgency. In the greater scheme of how He views man and the world as a whole, God requires of us to be in certain places at certain times so He can fulfill or begin something He wants to do. He was requiring us to get to this new country quickly for this very reason. He was up to something. Within six and a half short weeks of being shown that property by our new friends, we arrived to the magnificent wooded mountains of North Carolina. We stepped in to a spiritual prophetic hotbed populated by many diverse people doing the Lord's work in various ways and in various capacities. Again, we can see key people put in our path by the Lord to advance His purposes and plans through us; the Lord has a way of intersecting people for the carrying out of His plans in people's lives. This is a journey to be enjoyed, prayed through trusting that He has it under control. It's not by our might or devices of man; but by my Spirit, says the Lord. This *is* the word of the Lord to Zerubbabel (Zechariah 4:6, NKJV): "'Not by might nor by power, but by My Spirit,' says the LORD of hosts." Our new home proved to be built on prayer upon holy land; and thus, we arrived adding the anointing upon our lives to the land and displacing some spiritual giants that were at rest there. Shortly before our move, the Lord was inspiring us to build what I call Holy Ghost rest and restoration centers. The Lord gave Nancy and me both visions of what this would look like; and in our minds, we figured that this would happen way in the future, when we were much older. Well, upon arriving on our land in North Carolina, the Lord said, "I want you to begin here." Father God said to build some small, intimate log cabins on our property. He said to name them, Arks of His Testimony. He also said to build a worship room so the praise of His children would fill the air of the land, over the mountaintops and flow down to the valleys, soaking all the low places too. We even got ordained in our house on the holy mountain per the Lord's instructions. The Lord continues to expound upon and expand what we believe the definition of our ministry is expanding its scope to writing books, youth and adult alike, into the artistic world of dance, painting, and photography—as Nancy wrote her first visual devotional of many books to come forth. He wants His fullness to be better expressed, and that is what is lovely about the body of Christ. Each has its part to fulfill. Our part is the revealing of His heart (His love) to the world.

The rest and restoration center Arks of His testimony are yet to be fulfilled at the time of this writing yet remain fast in our hearts as deposited by the Lord. In fact, He has recently prompted us to relocate to Georgia to conduct our ministry.

The Heart of the Matter

As Recounted by Nancy

[Nancy's dialogue]

The Lord exchanged Matthew's heart for His own. I remember putting my hand on Matthew's chest while he was in the coma, and it felt different. I knew it was still Matthew's heart, but his heart was beating a different rhythm. I asked the nurses if, when Matthew flat-lined three times, that had anything to do with the different heartbeat I was feeling. They said no, looking at me with a questioning glance. I never received an answer; but deep in my heart, I always thought that God must have given Matthew a new heart, a new life. When Matthew is ministering, there is a direct line from the Lord like a supernatural pipeline directly connected to the heart of the Father to Matthew's. When Matthew hugs a man, for example, it is as if the Father

Himself is hugging them. Most times, they begin to weep because of the love of the Father that is going directly into their hearts. It is incredible. I remember on our first ministry trip overseas to England, France, and Italy, we were ministering in a small church in a fishing town, Pescara, in Italy. We needed an interpreter. As we finished speaking, we began to minister to the people with our interpreters at hand. Once Matthew began to hug the men and I hug the women, everyone was weeping. It was awesome how the Lord was flowing through us and ministering to their hearts in such a deep, intimate way. The Lord ministered to every person in that congregation. We are excited to go back and see the fruit of the Father in the people and their town. Abba Father is so in love with His children, He is always concerned for our *whole hearts*. Jeremiah 24:7 (NKJV): "And I will give them a heart to know (recognize, understand, and be acquainted with) Me, that I am the Lord; and they will be My people, and I will be their God, for they will return to Me with their *whole heart*." Psalm 9:1 (AMP): "I will praise You, O Lord, with my *whole heart*; I will show forth (recount and tell aloud) all Your marvelous works and wonderful deeds!" Deuteronomy 4:29 (NKJV): "But even there, if you seek God, your God, you'll be able to find him if you're serious, looking for him with your *whole heart* and soul." Deuteronomy 6:5 (MSG): "Love God, your God, with your whole heart; love him with all that's in you, love him with all you've got!" Deuteronomy 30:6 (MSG): "God, your God, will cut away the thick calluses on your heart and your children's hearts, freeing you to love God, your God, with your *whole heart* and soul and live, really live." 1 Chronicles 28:9 (MSG): "And you, Solomon my son, get to know well your father's God; serve him with a *whole heart* and eager mind, for God examines every heart and sees through every motive, If you seek him, he'll make sure you find him, but if you abandon him, he'll leave you for good."

Can you see a pattern here regarding the whole heart that Abba Father is concerned with? Daddy is exceedingly, abundantly in love with His children. In the Bible, there are several dozen scriptures regarding a whole heart, heart in general ripples throughout the pages of God's promises; words; and through His Son, Jesus Christ. Here are some coin phrases: issues of the heart, stony heart, callused heart, hard heart, heart of the matter, heart of gold, Father's heart, childlike heart, tenderhearted, weak at heart, heartsick, heartfelt, lonely hearted, shot through the heart—you get the idea.

I just want to share a heart ministry experience that happened in England during a ministry trip. First, a month earlier, the Lord put *heavy on my heart* to start interceding for people who have bipolar disorder. Amazingly, all I saw in magazines and television commercials alike was this debilitating disorder. My heart was sick. I prayed every time a commercial or interview was airing that dealt with bipolar disorder. It was evident that this was heavy on Daddy's heart.

We arrived in England, Colchester at very dear friends of ours that pastor an up-and-coming church. We ministered our testimony, and I gave a word of wisdom (prophetic word). Then time came for ministering to the people. One of the first guys came up and said, "I have bipolar." My spirit leaped inside as I said, "You are the one I have been interceding for over a month. The Lord gave me no rest." So Matthew and I both put our hand on his heart, praying and prophesying; and then we broke the spirit of bipolar and prayed on his mind to have the mind of Christ Jesus. So next time, when a young guy came up to pray at a church in Georgia, I looked at him and said, "This is easy for God. I saw God firsthand heal someone with that disorder." God heals all disorders and diseases: "I can do all things through Christ who strengthens me" (Philippians 4:13, NKJV).

Lastly, I want to share with you my "whole heart" experience. I entered Matthew's ICU room eighteen years ago with a whole heart of love for my husband for his life. "Lord bring back my husband, the heart of who he is, his personality and I promise to stay with him, even if he's in a wheelchair." That was a wholehearted cry that our Abba Father could not deny.

FAITH

[Matthew's dialogue]

In Hebrews 11:1, NKJV, we find a very commonly quoted scripture reading, "Now faith is the substance of things hoped for, the evidence of things not seen." I hear people all the time say things like, "Oh, just have faith," or, "If you only had faith ... " I guess my question then is just what is this faith that is thrown around like two baseball players warming up in the dugout before the big game? It's said that faith is like a mustard seed because that is the power behind it. It isn't a matter of having a lot or being big in order for it to activate God to move on your behalf. The mustard seed is a very small seed, about two millimeters in diameter yet grows to a large size. The growth of a mustard seed is said to be very powerful and persistent when growing. Romans 12:3 (NKJV), speaks, "For I say, through the grace given to me, to everyone who is among you, not to think of himself more highly than he ought to think, but to think soberly, as God has dealt to each one *a measure of faith* (italics mine)." So what we have here is having a glimmer of faith, having a glimmer of belief that God can do what He says is all we need. And keeping the hope in Him keeps watering and feeding that seed, with trust being the ground it's planted in.

I have been accused many times to my face and behind my back of not having enough faith for healing to manifest in my life. All I can say is that Jesus provided for my full healing by taking those horrendous stripes upon His back to the cross, dying on my behalf and being resurrected three days later to ascend to the Father in Heaven. There is nothing I personally can add to what He has already done and completed outside of believing in and loving Him. The Son of God completed the restoration process by making a way for us to have fellowship with God the Father giving us power through the Holy Spirit to bring more kids to the Father's kingdom, rescuing them from the kingdom of this world of darkness. For His is the kingdom of light. It is Christ in me, the hope of glory. He does the glorifying. He does the healing. He even provides the faith.

There are no formulas. Just believe God is Who He says He is. That's why we've been stressing that the most important thing is to know God at the experiential levels, to be intimate with the Trinity, to know the Holy Spirit's voice, to know all the different ways He communicates with you, and to remember that Jesus said, "He will never leave you nor forsake you (Joshua

1:5, NKJV).” That’s a pretty good deal from the Son of God that created everything you know and everything you don’t know. I say trust Him. We do.

“So if hope is the water for the seed, how do I remain hopeful when my world all around me is falling apart?” you ask. Well, as that most often quoted scripture mentions, “The evidence not yet seen,” means you are not able to see what is being orchestrated to bring about that thing which you are having faith for. Whether you believe it or not, we are living in a world that is even supernatural in origin. That means there are forces affecting the very world we live in on a day-to-day basis that are above or beyond what we see. Hebrews chapter 11, verse 3, NKJV, says, “By faith we understand that the worlds were framed by the word of God, so that the things which are seen *were not made of things which are visible* (italics mine).” Natural can be defined as something that exists in nature that is visible with our naked eyes. *Super* means over, above, or beyond that which we see as the natural. Remember, God always turns around that which was meant for evil to good. In Romans 8:28 (NKJV) we read, “And we know that all things work together for good to those who love God, to those who are the called according to His purpose.” Look at Genesis chapter 50, verses 19 and 20 (NKJV): “Joseph said to them, ‘Do not be afraid, for *am* I in the place of God? But as for you, you meant evil against me; *but* God meant it for good, in order to bring it about as *it is* this day, to save many people alive.’” I’m the perfect example in this turning around that God does. Getting shot in the head is definitely a bad thing, but God is turning it into something I can view as good (not the incident itself, but what it has led us to today).

"And we know that all things work together for good to those who love God, to those who are the called according to His purpose" (Romans 8:28, NKJV).

It's like you have to give Him a chance; and on His timetable, a day is like a thousand years and a thousand years a day to Him. 2 Peter 3:8–9 (NKJV): "But, beloved, do not forget this one thing, that with the Lord one day is as a thousand years, and a thousand years as one day." And verse 9 continues, "The Lord is not slack concerning His promise, as some count slackness, but is longsuffering toward us, not willing that any should perish but that all should come to repentance." He's speaking to gathering more of His kids to His kingdom before the last day; however, this shows that His schedule is His schedule to do what He desires to do, to do the turning around. Trust Him and His schedule. Like I said, I still don't like the fact that I have a 9 mm bullet in my head and left side paresis; but I would not change one thing about it if it meant I would not have met my Father the way I have and the working in my heart the way He is. I have faith that God will do what He has said He will do, even—and this is often the case—when I do not fully understand His ways.

I believe that remaining hopeful in bad times has a lot to do with perspective. By what perspective are you looking at your situation? And whose perspective are you viewing it through? It's tough to get outside of yourself when you're the one being affected by the situation. Believe me when I say that I know what it is like all these years dealing with my present situation. But we have to shift our perspective from what we think about our situation to what our heavenly Father thinks about it. I'll guarantee you one thing. He's thinking differently about it than you are. We read in 1 Corinthians 2, verses 9–12, "But as it is written: 'Eye has not seen, nor ear heard, nor have entered into the heart of man the things which God has prepared for those who love Him.' But God has revealed them to us through His Spirit, for the Spirit searches all things. Yes. The deep things of God. For what man knows the things of a man except the spirit of the man which is in him? Even so, no one knows the things of God except the Spirit of God. Now we have received not the spirit of the world, but the Spirit who is from God, that we might know the things that have been freely given to us by God." To sum that up, no one can know the Spirit of God, the mysteries, the deep things of God except the Spirit of God. In order to know the true view of a situation, we must therefore know God and have His Spirit, the Holy Spirit. Only then did I begin to learn to appreciate my situation. I'm not appreciating the bullet in my head. No. I'm appreciating what I'm learning from having a bullet in my head because I'm forced to seek His perspectives and not my own. That's how to remain hopeful and water those seeds of faith. You'll be amazed at what grows when we do things His way. Our ways are shortsighted and self-centered. His ways are other-centered; and by operating in love for others, your needs and desires will be fulfilled. He is a good God. Have faith in Him.

HOPE

AS RECOUNTED BY MATTHEW

[Matthew's dialogue]

What is hope? Wikipedia refers to hope as a belief in a positive outcome related to events and circumstances in one's life. Psalm 42:5 (NKJV) says hope in God. Psalm 39:7 (NKJV) speaks of having my hope in the Lord. Ephesians 1:18 (NKJV) speaks of knowing what the hope of His calling is, knowing what the riches of the glory of His inheritance in the saints are. This hope is God, the Father's hope, the riches of His inheritance in the saints. This put a whole new spin on the word *hope* for me when I realized that hope is not reserved for mankind only but the Father of all creation has hope. His hope is that not one should perish but that all might come unto Him through His Son, Jesus, the resurrected One. Hope includes such synonyms as *expectation*, *dream*, *plan*, *wish*, *prospect*, *likelihood*, *anticipate*. Hope is creative in nature. These are very powerful words that, when present, propel our lives forward, creating excitement, achievement, ingenuity, and resourcefulness in one's life. Their absence makes for a slow death through inactivity and lack of creativity and vision and will breed loneliness and seclusion. Why am I mentioning these various words? It is these very words that, fortunately for me, were not killed off by the tragic atrocity of being disabled at the young age of twenty-eight by a speeding bullet to the head eighteen years ago. Even while sitting low in a wheelchair, I had hope that I would one day walk again, hope that eventually I could stand in front of a toilet and go to the bathroom like I had been doing since getting out of diapers as a baby and being potty trained, hope that I would not need to be using that plastic jug for a urinal forever because of not being able to stand up, hope that one day I could drive again, hope that one day I would be able to be that husband my wife married once again. To this very day, I'm still hoping to be able to run. A lot has to happen for me physically for that type of coordination to be present, but I am holding fast to that hope of moving quickly—maybe just a jog at first. I'm hoping to someday not to have to wear a leg brace on my left leg and holding fast to my hope of using my left arm again. Our forward progress will stop right where our hope stops. Even against insurmountable odds, hope can rearrange things so that birthing can happen. Hope will put words of life on our tongues, for the heart of the man will be revealed by his tongue. Words of life spoken will affect your surrounding environment to better line up with your hopes. An interesting thing that I thought regarding the hope that I had before being shot was that we would build homes on a local lake, sell them to make money, and/or rent them to make money. The interesting part is that I still have hope of building upon land today but for a different purpose. Today's purpose is to create places where people can come to meet their God face to face. The rental of these various cabins still presents itself too. It's just that I serve a different Master today. Today, I serve God Almighty and not myself as mighty. And I still retain the hope of being the husband that my wife deserves. The only difference today is that the role I'm emulating is that of Jesus. Ephesians 5:25–26 (NKJV) says, "Husbands, love your wives, just as Christ also loved the church and gave Himself for her, so that He might sanctify and cleanse her with the washing of the word." Ephesians 5:28 (NKJV) goes on to say, "So husbands ought to love their wives as their own bodies; he who loves his wife loves himself." See the great importance placed on being in right standing with yourself? Imagine the road it was for me to come to grips with who I was after being shot. I don't want to repeat anything, for much has already been said about me coming to accept who I am after the injury; but you can see how important it was that I (came) come to the place of loving myself even in my disabled condition. Only after loving myself is it possible to love my wife. If I persisted in being unhappy with me, there is no way I could ever give her the happiness she deserves from a husband and best friend. It is impossible to give something to someone that you don't already have. I cannot give joy if I have not joy; I cannot give love if I have not love or if I'm centered on myself only.

I mentioned knowing the hope of His calling earlier. Once we know the hope of His calling, we can know the hope of our own calling because knowing our hope of our calling directly affects our activity in this life on a day-to-day basis. Jesus came to gather that which was lost and then asked us to continue harvesting that which is lost to Him. The great commission to go make disciples of all the nations, baptizing them in the name of the Father and of the Son and of the Holy Spirit (Mark 28:19–20, NKJV). There's a relationship between hope, vision, and trust.

Where does hope come from? How do we lose it? We lose it by believing in our circumstances, by what we see in the present moment, by what we feel rather than what we believe to be the truth. Who's truth? God's truth, for His truth is the only standard, the only truth that will never change. Apostle Paul, addressing the church in Rome, wrote in Romans 15:13 (NKJV), "Now may the God of hope fill you with all joy and peace in believing, that you may abound in hope by the power of the Holy Spirit." So, looking at this single scripture, I see that the power of the Holy Spirit is providing us hope and also that God Himself is of hope. Romans chapter 15 (NKJV), verse 4 says that through the patience and comfort of scriptures we might have hope. Using the Apostle Paul again, he, in 1 Thessalonians verse 8 (NKJV), refers to the helmet of salvation as our hope. It occurred to me that a helmet is worn on our heads and inside our physical head is our mind, which is what we think with. So, as Philippians 4:8, NKJV, says, "Whatever things are true, whatever things are noble, whatever things are just, whatever things are pure, whatever things are lovely, whatever things are of good report, if there is any virtue and if there is anything praise worthy—meditate on these things." This is not usually something that comes naturally to most people, especially in the midst of tribulation or tragedy; yet if one trains themselves to meditate on the hope of His calling, which has to do with not one of us being lost to the evil one of this current world and perishing, but having eternal life with Him, then it is ultimately going to be a good day. For if I myself looked upon my circumstances and accepted them as the final outcome, I would not have participated in one rehabilitative session because why should I? I would not wake up each morning eager to hear the wind or the birds and see my wife, for I wouldn't be a proverbial happy camper if I allowed that single 9 mm speeding bullet to dictate the outcome of my life. No. I believe there is always something worthy of praise.

Love is a word we hear and use a lot and in a variety of ways. Love, as defined via the online resource Dictionary.com, speaks of a profoundly tender, passionate affection for another person or a feeling of warm, personal attachment or deep affection, as for a parent, child, or friend; or even a sexual passion or desire. Some quotations regarding love are as follows.

> I never knew how to worship until I knew how to love.
> Henry Ward Beecher
> There is no remedy for love but to love more.
> Thoreau
> Spread love everywhere you go: first of all in your own house. Give love to your children, to your wife or husband, to a next door neighbor … Let no one ever come to you without leaving better and happier. Be the living expression of God's kindness; kindness

> in your face, kindness in your eyes, kindness in your smile, kindness in your warm greeting.
> Mother Theresa
> To know someone here or there with whom you can feel there is understanding in spite of distances or thoughts expressed; that can make life a garden.
> Goethe

We see quotes of all sorts about love, but I write of agape love, the love of God, for that is the love that pulled me from the depths of hell. Agape love is that which is unconditional; for example, I love the men who shot me, regardless of how violently they harmed me and, subsequently, my wife. Friendship love, or phileo love, is something that is conditional and emotional. (Believe me. If by my emotions I were to address this issue of life, I would be miserable.) Romans 12:10 (NKJV) speaks of brotherly love: "Be kindly affectionate to one another with brotherly love, in honor giving preference to one another." That's phileo love. We truly can say that we have love for the perpetrators because we've chosen to operate in agape love.

"Let love be without hypocrisy, Abhor what is evil. Cling to what is good" (Romans 12:9, NKJV).

We've got a hard enough time loving ourselves. We're such a visually oriented society concerned, obsessed with appearances, namely our own. If it weren't for the agape love, I most certainly would be my own enemy.

Phileo love, a kind of conditional, potentially with strings attached, love, may not have been able to handle myself in my newfound handicapped situation surely resulting in anger and generally just being a miserable person. Of course, I preferred myself in the physically strong and muscularly attractive state I was in before my injury. Who wouldn't prefer that? However, if loving myself and my happiness depended on that alone, then there would be no peaceful existence in my life. I would be living a life full of regrets consumed with thoughts of what I had lost. I would imagine that if my wife's love hinged solely on my physical appearances and attributes, she too would have been miserable with me or left me altogether. It's like Adam and Eve in the garden of Eden; satan got Eve to look more at what she didn't have rather than the blessings that she did have, and Adam followed suit eating of the fruit.

It's no wonder divorce is as rampant in America today, as this agape love is rare. Agape love says, "I don't care what you may have done wrong in the past or what you're presently doing; I love you right where you are." Agape love is full of unconditional sacrifice. That means I am going to do something for you that you yourself cannot do for yourself; and I'm going to do it without any strings attached, without any expectation of your actions. That's what God did giving His Son up to die on the cross to cover our sins. John 3:16 (NKJV): "For God so loved the world that he gave his one and only Son, that whoever believes in Him shall not perish but have eternal life." He did so without any expectations or requirements on our behalf. Romans 5:8 (NKJV): "But God demonstrates his own love for us in this: While we were still sinners, Christ died for us." Matthew 22:14 (NKJV): "For many are called, but few are chosen." He won't violate our free will to make a choice. He will call us, but it's up to us to answer that call. He desires that all come to Him to be saved. 1 Timothy 2:4 (NKJV) says, "Who desires all men to be saved and to come to the knowledge of the truth." And once we answer that call, we get the rest of the package: the Father, Son, and Holy Spirit and eternal life in the kingdom of God. Agape love, as described in 1 Corinthians chapter 13, verses 4–7 (NKJV), reads:

> Suffers long and is kind; love does not envy; love does not parade itself, is not puffed up; does not behave rudely, does not seek its own, is not provoked, thinks no evil; does not rejoice in iniquity, but rejoices in the truth; bears all things, believes all things, hopes all things, endures all things.

These things all operate outside of oneself. Agape love is a fruit of the Spirit. Galatians 5:22 (NKJV) reads, "But the fruit of the Spirit is love, joy, peace, longsuffering, kindness, goodness, faithfulness ..." Without the Holy Spirit in us, this love is impossible. We must accept and know that Holy Spirit is here with us and in us. He didn't leave yet. Jesus told us that He, the Helper, would come if He went away. Jesus did His part by making a way for all of us to the Father, absolving us of our sins; and He left us Helper too.

Find the place in your heart so that when you look at the person in the supermarket line, you can look at them and love them because they are from the same Maker of the universe, God Almighty, whether they know it or not.

[Nancy's dialogue]

Imagine Matthew and I married only three years, both having successful jobs, and the roles of husband and wife were balanced. He takes care of the outside and I take care of the inside with equal decision making of financial areas like large purchases and investments alike. Our goals were to buy on the lake a fixer-upper and move in and rent out our first home that we just remodeled in January 1992.

We both worked hard and loved outside activities like rollerblading, boating, skiing, hiking, golf, and jet skiing—fun in the sun sports.

In only a split second, our entire life disappeared and turned upside down.

Everything was stripped away, like when someone has the wind knocked out of them but forever. All that Matthew and I worked for was gone; everything we thought that was important vanished. What remained was the sole responsibility of everything put upon my shoulders—decisions, therapies, financial, healthcare, being the caregiver, being the only one who could make the decisions for our life and beyond. From the moment of being touched by Jesus, my Father Abba, Daddy, knew that His Son imparted into me strength, anointing, peace, joy, love, kindness longsuffering, self-control, patience. I got the entire package in working order from day one. When someone gives his or her life over to the Lord, salvation, the journey begins discovering who you are in Christ and who Christ is in you, so you *receive* the entire package, inheritance, promises of His covenant. Believe me. I truly needed everything up and running for the road we had to travel. Salvation is only the beginning, and discovering the new life of a supernatural lifestyle and discovering the promises and access to the Father Himself with all the benefits, ultimately meeting Father Abba Daddy. Intimacy means knowing that you are the son or daughter of the Most High and all the authority and legal rights of royalty are yours.

Here I am carrying the world on my shoulders, plus we had incredible support team—family, friends, therapies, and doctors all helped us chart these unknown waters.

As Matthew regained more of his cognitive skills, there were times that he would help with decisions regarding therapies alike. One of the biggest gains in decision making was when we were moving to Florida. He was more cognitive; and Matthew was beginning to take on the role of a husband again, but some areas like the checkbook and paying bills were not so good.

With the type of brain injury, the higher executive skills came later on, like planning, structured activities, etc. Matthew needed a lot more down time to rest his brain.

Ephesians 5:31 (NKJV) says, "For this reason a man shall leave his father and mother and be joined to his wife, and the two shall become one flesh." I took this very seriously as Matthew laid in his coma, not knowing if he would make it through the night. The odious feeling was that I could not feel Matthew; the connection was gone. I *felt nothing* until I was touched by Jesus and went back into Matthew's room and said, "Lord bring back my husband bring back who he is, his heart, his personality, and I promise to stay with him even if he is in a wheelchair." I could not feel the connection, the bond, because Matthew was in hell until I asked God to bring him back; then I felt reconnected. A marriage covenant is the strongest bond you can have between a man and a woman.

In the Bible, the Word of God, the sword, God is clear and straightforward.

> Wives, submit to your own husbands, as to the Lord. For the husband is head of the wife, as also Christ is head of the church; and He is the Savior of the body. Therefore, just as the church is subject to Christ, so let the wives be to their own husbands in everything. Husbands, love your wives, just as Christ also loved

> the church and gave Himself for her, that He might sanctify and cleanse her with washing of water by the word, that He might present her to Himself a glorious church, not having spot or wrinkle or any such thing, but that she should be holy and without blemish. So husbands ought to love their own wives as their own bodies; he who loves his wife loves himself. For no one ever hated his own flesh, but nourishes and cherishes it, just as the Lord does the church; for we are members of His body, of His flesh and of His bones.
>
> Ephesians 5:22–30 (NKJV)

Let me tell you all the fruit of God's covenant of marriage in our lives. We have been happily married for twenty-one years. Spiritually, I am covered by my husband. He prays for me, over me, and waters me with the Word of God. I respect Matthew. I submit. Yes, we talk about situations; but Matthew has the final say. Talk about a load off my shoulders. There is incredible peace in that I am able to walk in who I am; a daughter of the Most High, with all my gifts; an ordained minister, a loving wife, a dedicated caregiver, and a passionate lover. Being in full submission to my husband enables me to be who I am but, most of all, walk in the true covenant of God, true inheritance, and all benefits of a holy wife in God's eyes.

So I challenge you to stop shortchanging your marriage. Men, be the head; and love your wife as Christ loves the church. Women, submit fully and respect your husband and you will see fruitfulness immediately. Test

God on this one and see the love flow from your hearts once again.

"This is a great mystery, but I speak concerning Christ and the church. Nevertheless let each one of you in particular so love his own wife as himself, let the wife see that she respects her husband," (Ephesians 5:32–33, NKJV).

[Matthew's dialogue]

I remember many instances where my progress seemed to be taking forever; yet somehow I knew to be thankful for where I was at, thankful that I had enough short-term memory to be able to recall extreme difficulties from the month before and now instead of extreme insurmountable difficulties, I faced them as challenges. And when defined as challenges, that had an ability to take the edge off, so to speak, so I could remain thankful for where I was and what I had already done. A thankful heart inside of me made/makes me weepy, tearful because of the compassion that wells up for all that has been done for me. So many times would come (and still do come) that I cannot even speak or look at my wife, for example, because I get wracked with tears of gratitude for what she's done for me. To this day, I cannot read John 19:30 (NKJV), when Jesus says, "It is finished," because I have such a deep understanding and gratitude for what He did for me it tears me up inside to meditate on such a sacrifice. *True gratitude will focus your attention beyond the gift to that of the Giver.* I knew that God Almighty had pulled me from the very depths of hell. I was set free by the hand of God to live once again; and I had the choice to live it as I desired, yet I eventually learned that I would not live it as I pleased but as He pleased, for He was the Giver of life, He was the Returner of my life. He could have very well left me in the pits of hell 'till judgment day cometh; but no, He didn't. He pulled me out. So it's hard to remain or get upset at somebody (God) who has done such a great thing for me. And He will do great things for you. Gratitude can take you from where you presently are to someplace you're supposed to be in the future, for gratitude is a vehicle, a key even, based on thankfulness and appreciation to bring you into your future. Gratitude is infectious; it's contagious. It affects those around you. It brings the best out in others because you are valuing them for who they are and even what they are doing. Gratitude will tend to get you favor from those surrounding you. Having gratitude and being thankful always got me favor from the therapists working with me in ways that they would go the extra mile in helping me rebuild my body, mind, and life. Gratitude is organic in nature; and it came out of me in a very genuine, real way that changed the environment. I say organic in that it occurred naturally from within me. It wasn't something that I had to contrive or muster up; it was intrinsic in nature and thus seemed to make the whole environment I was involved in work together for maximum efficiency.

I am grateful for my right arm so I can type these very words. (Yes, my left is still partially paralyzed, hemi-paresis.) Being gratuitous for the sacrifices my wife chose to make, without repetition of her numerous activities, I'll highlight just a few here—like chauffeuring me around everywhere for those many years I couldn't drive; pushing me around in my wheelchair; most importantly, her putting all her desires and wants as a person, as a woman, and as a wife on hold or laying them down entirely are all aspects that I was thankful for and continue to be thankful for to this day. I can only speculate as to how negative the effects would have been upon my life if Nancy had not sacrificed everything for me. Gratitude created an atmosphere of shared victories for me as well as shared losses. It's always better to have support in the down times, and it's just more fun to have support around to celebrate victories with. Gratitude flows from a humble heart, a meek and contrite Spirit; teachable in all my ways. There's a whole host of scriptural references found throughout the Bible on the few words I've written above—*meek*, *humble*, *contrite*, *teachable*—and all are necessary for sincere gratitude to exist and for true reconciliation of mind, body, and soul. Meekness refers to showing mildness and quietness of nature. Humbleness refers to feeling and/or showing respect and deference toward others. The Bible says in Matthew 5:5 (NKJV) that the meek shall inherit the earth. "Blessed are the meek, for they shall inherit the earth." Why would it say that, and what does that have to do with me?" you might ask. Meekness is a quality in a person that makes the person usable by God. The opposite of meek is proud or arrogant, and God says He resists the proud. James 4:6 (NKJV): "God resists the proud, but gives grace to the humble." I certainly needed grace to be able to deal with my newfound disability and continue to need more and more of it each day. I know that, biblically speaking, some of you might be saying, "But grace is God's way to cover our sin." "Moreover the law entered that the offense might abound. But where sin abounded, grace abounded much more, so that as sin reigned in death, even so grace might reign through righteousness to eternal life through Jesus Christ our Lord," (Romans 5:20–21, NKJV). And, yes, praise the Lord for His abundant grace for our sins to be forgiven. As Apostle Paul stated, we certainly would be dead in our sin rather than being able to reign in life through Jesus. The Apostle Peter says (2 Peter 3:9, NKJV), "The Lord is not slack concerning His promise, as some count slackness, but is longsuffering toward us, not willing that any should perish but that all should come to repentance." It is only by His grace that such is possible that more people might come to know Him.

But another facet of grace I'm speaking of is defined in Encarta's dictionary: "a capacity to tolerate, accommodate, or forgive people." I especially have need of *tolerate* and *accommodate* with regard to my newfound situation. So, why would He resist the proud? The proud are often self-righteous, not teachable; and as a fallen race of humans, through the acts of Adam and

Eve, we need to be taught by God how to rule and reign on Earth as He commanded us to in Genesis 1:28 (NKJV): "Then God blessed them, and God said to them, 'Be fruitful and multiply; fill the earth and subdue it; have dominion over the fish of the sea, over the birds of the air, and over every living thing that moves on the earth.'" The Apostle Paul wrote in Colossians 3:12 (NKJV): "Therefore, as *the* elect of God, holy and beloved, put on tender mercies, kindness, humility, meekness, longsuffering," in describing the character of the new man, one who has received Christ.

Colossians 3:17 (ERV): "Everything you say and everything you do should all be done for Jesus your Lord (Master). And in all you do, give thanks to God the Father through Jesus." I heard it said that gratitude is the root of joy. I think that is pretty appropriate, especially when combined with learning to appreciate what we have around us because then that is exactly what ends up filling us—appreciation and gratitude for all life and for where we are presently in life. "And in all you do give thanks …" It's easy to see why I am thankful and grateful for every day I get now after being in hell for a day and comatose for twenty-seven days. That's a long time, a big chunk of my life removed by a bad choice on someone else's behalf that is having lifelong consequences. Thank God for *His* choice and it's immediate and eternal consequences for *me*.

[Matthew's dialogue]

This is an often-quoted phrase in society today descriptive of something that scarred an individual beyond that which they expected—the problem being that I don't think many folks really know what they're talking about. They picked up the saying because of what they may have read in the Bible or been taught in Sunday school as a kid or seen in a movie or read in a horror novel or even seen in a comic as a kid. All of those don't hold a proverbial match to actually experiencing hell for real, of going to the place of eternal torment for you all by yourself. For those of you who think you're just gonna continue in your fun-loving, over the top partying practices, I've got news for you. There's no party going on down there. The fun and games of the party life you think you have on earth you will not have there. Hell has no fun in it. It wasn't designed to have fun in it. It was created for the fallen angels that rebelled with Lucifer against God in heaven thousands of years ago. It doesn't even make sense (by any stretch of the imagination) that God would create a place where a person could have fun while the whole time on earth they are going against God's will by doing the perversities that some do by not acknowledging that God sent His one and only Son, Jesus, to be put to death on a cross after a horrible scourging with a whip that we cannot truly imagine the pain of. Don't you think that God would require something of us after such a huge sacrifice on His part? He's asking that we be obedient to what He directs, for He is the Author and Finisher of all that we know. He knows the beginning and the end; therefore, what He says is definitely the right way for us to follow. It's just that, as the Word says, our flesh is enmity against the things of the Spirit and will not be subject to the Spirit; therefore, it's through our choice that we determine to subject the flesh to the Spirit, meaning do as we hear the Father do. Just as Jesus said to His disciples, "He does only what He sees the Father do and says only what He hears the Father say. It sounds simple enough until you try to put it into practice on a daily basis while living on this planet called Earth in these mortal bodies. It comes down to issues of the heart. Issues of the heart will set your course in life. Issues of the heart will dictate your actions; likewise, your destination will be determined by the same issues of heart. That's why it's imperative that the heart is right and set on the right things.

Why would He reach into hell for me? It's actually quite simple: because my wife asked Him to.

[Matthew's dialogue]

The past has always shown a person that is saved but remains unhealed, as the individual surely is their own cause for the disability and certainly the case if the disability remains once finding salvation. The person must have sin in his or her life or his or her faith isn't big enough or maybe he or she is not praying right. I don't think it's that cut and dry. Sin certainly can keep a person in bondage. And if you have faith as big as a mustard seed, Jesus says it's big enough; and if you're talking to God from your heart as a child would, what better way to pray. So, let's speak to the person, to his or her heart that comes in with the disability, not focusing on the disability and stigmatizing the person point blank. I myself, a person with a disability in the church, am guilty of this very thing. I often see a person in a wheelchair and instantly conclude that they need healing and that they surely must want prayer for their healing. Thoughts racing through my mind include, "Jesus healed them all … ," and, "We're to do greater works than He … " The Leviticus priests, those who were allowed into the most holy of holies to minister before the Lord, were to be unblemished, without any defect (Leviticus 21:17–23, NKJV). That old covenant law ruled out any person with a disability ministering before the Lord. Huh. But when Jesus arrived on the scene, He began doing things from the inside out, not outside, i.e., physical capacity or incapacities or appearances. He began on the inside, in the heart of the person. Let's love the person entering church right where they are.

Fortunately for us, today, we do not have to make burnt animal offerings before the Lord; but we are ourselves living sacrifices (Romans 12:1–2, NKJV). About one fifth of the world's population is disabled. So how does one reconcile their healing or lack thereof with the Lord's words?

Now there's a conundrum for those, like myself, who continue in disability because the Lord is Who He says He is, Jehovah Rapha, translated, "I am the Lord that healeth thee," and that never changes. He will always be the One that heals all my infirmities, regardless of myself. He heals because He is love, pure love. He is Jehovah Nissi, translated as, "I am the Lord our banner over thee." He is Jehovah Jireh, translated, "I am the Lord the provider for thee." The Lord knows the number of hairs on our heads and he knows what we need before we even know it. Jehovah Shamma is translated, "the Lord is present." The Lord will never not be around, especially when we think we're alone in our darkest hours. He always has His eyes on His children. I am starting to think that I have less to do with it than I ever thought. I once was taught that I've got a lot of the burden on my own shoulders, not an easy yoke to carry, regarding my own healing. Jesus does tell us over and over that His yoke is easy and light; so, in essence, it's my perceived yoke of healing that can drag me down to the ground in defeat, not yielding to the Christlike character that I am to exemplify while in this world. Jesus said that He did not come to rescue us from this world but to keep the evil one away from us.

Jesus prays in John 17:13–21 (NKJV):

> But now I come to You; and these things I speak in the world so that they may have My joy made full in themselves. I have given them Your word; and the world has hated them, because they are not of the world, even as I am not of the world. I do not ask You to take them out of the world, but to keep them from the evil *one.* They are not of the world, even as I am not of the world. Sanctify them in the truth; Your word is truth. As You sent Me into the world, I also have sent them into the world. For their sakes I sanctify Myself, that they themselves also may be sanctified in truth.
>
> I do not ask on behalf of these alone, but for those also who believe in Me through their word; that they may all be one; even as You, Father, *are* in Me and I

> in You, that they also may be in Us, so that the world may believe that You sent Me.

Verse 23 goes on to say, "I in them and You in Me, that they may be perfected in unity, so that the world may know that You sent Me, and loved them, even as You have loved Me." Maybe "perfected in unity" means that we need each other, especially with all our differences, in order to reach perfection. The next time you encounter someone with a handicap, genuinely welcome them with warm hugs, loving them right where they are, and let them decide what they want and when they want it. If you encounter them in a prayer line, sincerely ask them what they want and what they're there for. Maybe they don't even want prayer for themselves but are there in proxy for someone else. Ask the Lord what He says about the person. And then tell them what the Lord says. Treat them as you would like to be treated. This will lead to folks being more conscious of other people's feelings.

MOST FREQUENTLY ASKED QUESTIONS

WHY DIDN'T I ASK FOR HELP?

[Matthew's dialogue]

I hate that question. I'd spent all twenty-eight of my life years learning and mastering the art of self-reliance, which is especially true of the male species. We are looked upon for strength, leadership, protection, provision, companionship, propagation, and meeting needs. We, as kids growing up, start lifting weights so we can get bigger and stronger; and some of us even decide to start eating the right foods that can enhance the process. We get involved in physical sport activities to show off our prowess as a man or men, be it in single, one-on-one, "I can beat you," competition or in teams of, "We can beat you." So how, in a split second, am I supposed to figure out how to ask for help when, for all of my adult life, I've learned to do it on my own? What does a child learn but to walk and talk and all the cognitive motor functions society expects him or her to learn on his or her way to adulthood.

In an instant, I was knocked down from standing on my own two feet to sitting on two wheels … from looking straight into people's eyes with my head held high to looking straight at their waist and being looked down at because now I am seated lower than all adults. Having to endure the public ask my wife what I want because since I'm in a wheelchair and injured-looking I must not be cognizant of what's going on, much less be intelligent. I learned quickly what it meant to be judged by appearances of a handicap. Talk about a blow to my pride. That's one of the most difficult aspects as a man to have dealt with and still be dealing with to a certain degree at differing times. I think one of the reasons I can be at a point in my life that I can ask for help (sometimes) is that I remember all that I have accomplished and all that I've been forced to walk through since becoming injured. Every day, there is something that I have to overcome—either physically referenced or mentally oriented. I still get stared at because of the leg brace I wear on my left leg and the stiffness in which I walk.

How do you reconcile the past to the present?

[Matthew's dialogue]

What does reconciliation mean? It is the act of reconciling, which means to settle or resolve; to bring oneself to accept, to reestablish a close relationship, (Colossians 1, 2, Corinthians 5 NKJV). These Bible verses refer to how God reconciled the world to Himself, but what about those with an acquired disability? How do they reconcile the now-injured self with the image of themselves before the injury? Is it as simple as a matter of choice? Like God suggested in Deuteronomy 30 to choose life and good or death and evil? Is it as simple as saying to oneself, "I am going to choose life and good today"? Does that simple decision then begin to align one's life toward happiness and fulfillment? I think there is an apparent difference to be considered in terms of onset. Is it slow, over long periods of time, as in the normal aging process that makes it easier for a person to accept the physical and cognitive decline, or are we talking about the split-second scenario of injury onset like mine? I think injuries that happen suddenly create a much more difficult scenario to deal with than the slow decline many experience in aging today.

Do I Forgive Myself?

[Matthew's dialogue]

It wasn't until just a few years ago that I understood that that question pertained to me. While at a PIH (Partners in Harvest), a gathering of pastors and leaders associated with TACF (Toronto Airport Christian Fellowship), I was asked if I had forgiven myself. I recall standing amongst a group of my peers, not fully knowing how to respond. I knew in my heart at that point that I needed to forgive myself in my heart. After that, my brain caught on, realizing the validity of the question. I was holding myself responsible. Not that I was angry or frustrated at myself, but I needed to let myself be free of holding any responsibility for this tragic event. I've always believed that we are a product of choices that we make. We have a lot to do with the walking out of our own God-given destinies. "Choose this day that you will serve … ," (Joshua 24:15, NKJV). I was raised being taught that we should be held responsible for our actions, which are correct; and even God's Word backs that assumption up. But to assume the responsibility for the shooting upon my shoulders is a faulty thought process. As I outlined earlier, there were choices made from the tree of knowledge (satan's realm); and that wrought the death and destruction we experienced.

I've taken the liberty of interlinking these two concepts/processes—adapting and forgiving—for it seems that you can't have one without the other. When you forgive someone, you are, in essence, adapting. For twenty-eight years, I put together what I determined to be "my life," forming who I was, assembling my ego states based on the world I lived in, and interacting with a society void of personal handicap or disability. I grew up learning that I could do all things—or at least all things were possible for me to do. This pattern or plan for living is often referred to as a life script. So, the question begets, "Who am I now? What is my life script now?" As I write, thoughts are coming to me regarding all the sociological and psychological theories of how people become who they are as adults. The only thing that is mattering to me at the present as I contemplate what should be written—all I hear is the heart of the matter that matters in my heart: your heart. My heart never grew cold or dim in this life-altering event. Fortunately, Jesus had His way; and my heart seeks fast after Him to this day. Life scripts, a person's pattern or plan for living, come out of the heart of a person that has been formed and reformed into concrete responses, either good or bad, depending on the nature of the script's formation. Some say that up until six years of life a child is forming these behavioral scripts based on the human interactions and responses and behaviors around them; then, thereafter, they accept, reject, or reform them. Either way, cementation into the behavioral psyche occurs. So what does this mean for the ability to forgive a person when wronged? Jesus Christ instructs us to forgive those who have transgressed against us; for if we do not, how can our heavenly Father forgive us? How can we treat another with the love and respect that human beings deserve if, inside, our very heart is pain, anguish, remorse, or even revenge in its most bitter fashion? The only way we can truly love someone is by total, unconditional acceptance of who they are, supporting and edifying them for who they are, what they are doing, and what they feel is important. Faults are inherent in every person. The interesting thing inherent in judgment is that they, the judgments themselves, will play themselves out in a spouse or child or other interpersonal relationship or even through nature. The universe has a funny way of fulfilling the law of sowing and reaping. Christianity teaches us that God invented the law of sowing and reaping. 'Hear me then, my friends, as I say: Be not deceived. God is not mocked. "For whatsoever a man soweth, that shall he also reap," (Galatians 6:6–10, NKJV). It is written plainly in God's Word. It is proved by experience. I read that J. Wilbur Chapman once said regarding Galatians 6:7, "We shall reap if we sow. Sow a thought and you reap an act. Sow an act and you reap a habit. Sow a habit and you reap a character. Sow a character and you reap a destiny. It is written in God's Word that we shall reap what we sow."

How about forgiving God?

"What do you mean, or how about God?" you might ask.

[Mathew's dialogue] I'm referring to getting bitter with God Himself because I'm still disabled eighteen years post injury. I know some people (and I'll go ahead and include myself in this group) who, at one point or another, when an answer to prayer is not immediate in coming, start casting all sorts of undue judgments on God and on themselves. I might ask questions like, "What am I doing wrong?" We might even go so far as to form doctrine around a false assumption, like, "Obviously, God doesn't heal anymore," or "I'm not worthy," or "I'm not doing something right." First, healing is for today. (Remember, I'm penning this book, sitting before the keyboard, typing with only one hand because my left is still paralyzed.) We, as children of God, are all worthy of being healed. I believe it's really a matter of trust in the long-term disability manifestations, meaning that God's way is more interested in our hearts than anything else. And I for one totally trust that God knows what He's doing with my healing. I totally agree that all healing was done in the stripes of His Son, Jesus, back on the cross; and, therefore, by my mere acceptance of Jesus, I have all that healing inside of me. I don't think of myself as disabled. I dream fully healed. My visions include myself fully healed inside and out. So, my point in saying any of this is that it's impossible for me to become disappointed or bitter at Daddy for my current situation. And I'm not so proud that I don't continually ask Him to pour out His grace and mercy upon me and that He quickens to my spirit and heart all that He may wish me to know more or learn. One thing I know is that He's got an omniscient view; He sees all at once from beginning to end. So who are you going to trust? I trust that He's got the whole thing well in His hands, just like when He pulled me up out of the cell in hell.

Who was I to Who I am Now?

[Matthew's dialogue]

If God can reconcile the entire world to Him, don't you think we can reconcile ourselves with ourselves through Him? See, through Him, all things are possible. Through Him, not ourselves, for we certainly will fall short due to our limited capacities in and of ourselves. Maybe it's got to do with the pattern He established by putting His Son to death on the cross at Calvary. In saying that I mean it's the death and resurrection principle that applies here. I, for example, am dead to who I was as measured by my physical attributes and mental cognitions to being resurrected in Jesus. In Him I am a fully complete son of God. What else is there to achieve but to shake off the shackles of this world and enter His, regardless of ability or attribute. "There is therefore no condemnation to those who are in Christ Jesus, who do not walk according to the flesh, but according to the Spirit," (Romans 8:1, NKJV). This is a means of reconciliation with all of humanity, shaking off who we believe we are through our own or somebody else's eyes and gazing upon ourselves from our Father's eyes, regarding no one according to the flesh (2 Corinthians

5:16b, NKJV). "Therefore, if anyone is in Christ, he is a new creation; old things have passed away; behold all things have become new. Now all things are of God, who has reconciled us to Himself through Jesus Christ, and has given us the ministry of reconciliation," (2 Corinthians 5:17–18, NKJV). As I mentioned earlier regarding the definition of reconciliation in that "Bring oneself to accept and reestablish a close relationship …," this is something that I had to walk through regarding myself and how I viewed me; accepting who I am and where I am and reestablishing a close relationship with myself. One of the most important things I learned is to not accept the world's definition of who I am. It's my Father's view that's important to me, so just what is my Father's view of me? First off, since I did choose to believe in Jesus, I am now a saint in the kingdom of God (1 Corinthians 1:2, NKJV), which means I am set apart, dedicated and holy, no longer a sinner but one of God's elect in that He actually chose me first. It's basically impossible to choose God from our original decrepit, fallen state. It takes the Holy Spirit to make a house call and drop in the ability to believe in Him in the first place (Ephesians 1:4, NKJV). Being holy also means righteous and sacred. We actually receive praises from God because of our relationship with His Son (see Romans 2:29, NKJV). (See Romans 8:31–39, NKJV.) Jesus, seated by His Father God, makes intercession for us day and night; nothing can separate us from the love of God in Christ. And God justifies us, so who can be against us? Believe me. There are plenty of times experiencing the "against me" part via quick judgments, discrimination, and decisions that I've experienced in my journey through this injury. We are members of the household of God (Ephesians 2:19, Hebrews 3:6; NKJV). "Just as He chose us in Him before the foundation of the world, that we should be holy and without blame before Him in love, having predestined us to adoption as sons by Jesus Christ Himself, according to the good pleasure of His will (Ephesians 1:4–5, NKJV).

DID WE FORGIVE THE GUYS?

[Matthew's dialogue]

Just as automatic as the 9 mm Uzi machine gun that shot me was, so was our forgiveness toward the men bearing those weapons.

Our act of forgiveness toward them was not something we had to work up or find in ourselves through intellectual means. No. The forgiveness blossomed from deep in our hearts; and all we had to do was release it, thereby releasing ourselves to move forward from being the victims to victors.

AFTERWORD

[Nancy's dialogue]

"Fire one, baby. Fire one," will always be burned in my mind; and for Matthew, the bullet will be burned into his brain for the rest of our lives. Does that one split second set the course for our entire lives? No. The hand of God going into hell and the hand of Jesus pulling me back from darkness defines who we are: His Beloved.

So, you've read this book or just came across it and are perusing its contents and are thinking, *Hey, how can I know this Jesus you're talking about?* Well, it's quite simple, in fact. Romans 10: 9–10 (NKJV) says, "That if you confess the Lord Jesus with your mouth and believe in your heart that God has raised Him from the dead, you will be saved. For with the heart one believes unto righteousness, and with the mouth confession is made unto salvation." So those are the biblical salvation verses. Now, repeat after me: "Dear Lord Jesus, I believe that You are the One and only Son of God. I believe that You died on the cross and rose from the dead three days later to live forevermore. Jesus, please come into my heart. I'm sorry for my wrongdoings. I turn from those things that are evil, and I cling to You from here on out. *Holy Spirit*, I ask that You come and fill me to overflowing. Give me a new song in my heart that my mouth may worship You by. I ask for the heavenly language, the gift of tongues found in 1 Corinthians 12:10–11." Praise the Lord. You are now part of His kingdom, a child of God with eternal life and abundance from on high.

We've found that the onslaught of injury can open the door for various attacks from the enemy. Therefore, we'd like to suggest the following prayers to vanquish these doors. Pray the following verbally from your heart.

"Lord, I forgive those who have hurt me. I release them from holding them captive in my own mind to You, Lord. Please heal the hurt inside me to be healed, and I forgive them who hurt me and ask the healing balm of Gilead to saturate my heart and mind. I thank You."

Our physical bodies have, at the cellular level, the ability to remember what happened to us, good and bad; therefore, it is necessary to be freed at that level too.

"In the name of Jesus; I command all tissues to line up with the creative, life-giving Word of God. All trauma, go in the name of Jesus. I cut off all words of sickness and pain. All words of medical diagnosis, go. Be gone. All words of limitation I command are gone in Jesus's name. Mind, be renewed by the mighty, all-powerful Holy Spirit. I command all negative memories to be washed away into the sea of forgetfulness. Now go and immerse yourself in the Word of God. I speak life into your tissues and not death. I speak recovery and not stagnation into your body. Mind, line up with the Word of God. Be renewed in Christ, in the name of Jesus."

I command *joy* to be your strength from this day forward, *peace* to be your rear guard.

PHOTO GALLERY

Before Injury

Matthew and Nancy Before Injury

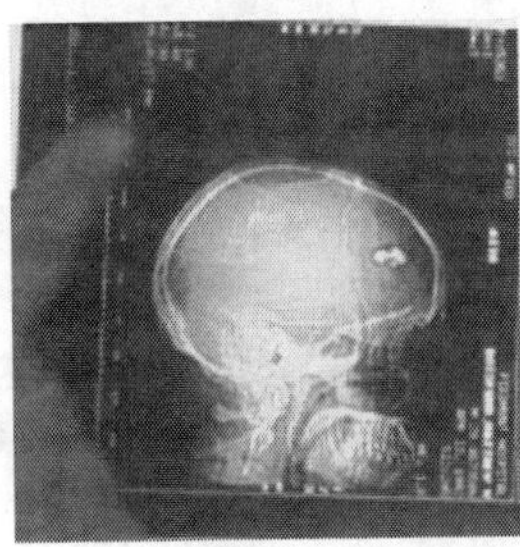

Catscan - Bullet in Head

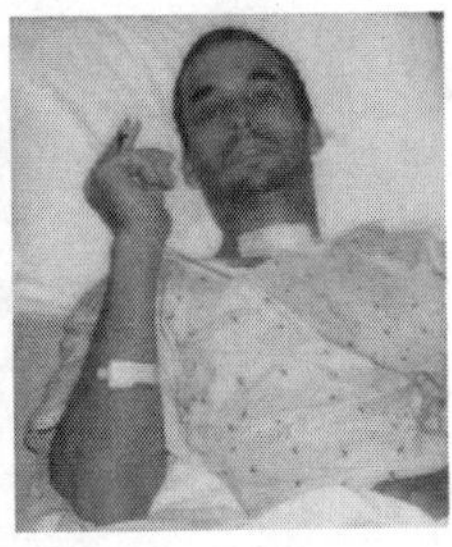

Coming Out of Coma

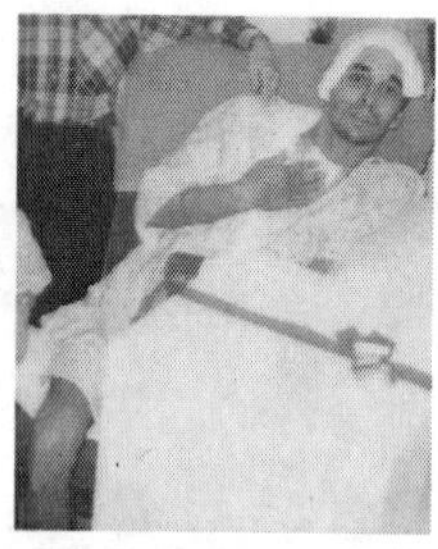

First Time Sitting

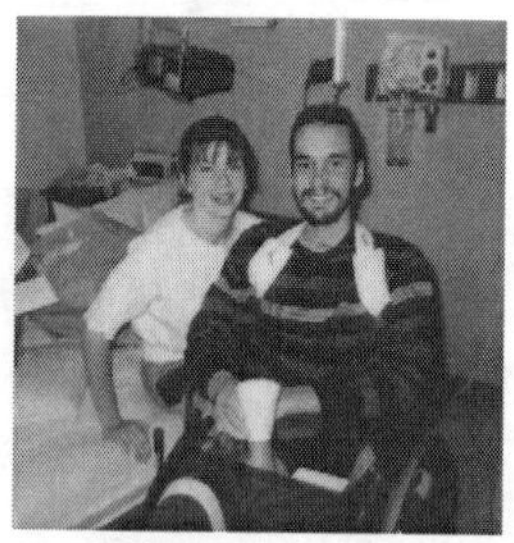

In Wheelchair At the Hospital

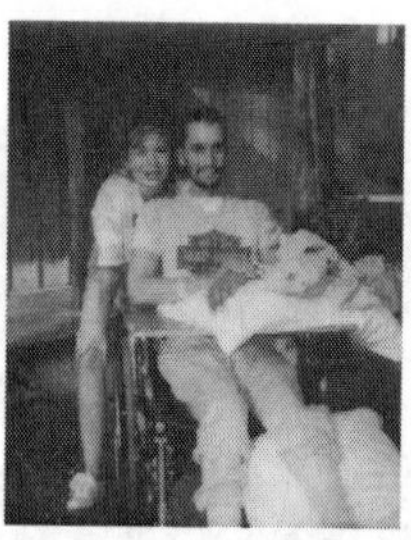

Home From Hospital

First Time Standing

Matthew and Nancy Botsford